Colin McCarty
Caroline Cooke

Progress in Understanding Mathematics Assessment

MANUAL STAGE 2

Years 3–6

RISING STARS ASSESSMENT

Hachette UK's policy is to use papers that are natural, renewable and recyclable products and made from wood grown in sustainable forests. The logging and manufacturing processes are expected to conform to the environmental regulations of the country of origin.

Orders: please contact Bookpoint Ltd, 130 Park Drive, Milton Park, Abingdon, Oxon OX14 4SE. Telephone: (44) 01235 400555. Fax: (44) 01235 400454. Email primary@bookpoint.co.uk. You can also order through our website: www.hoddereducation.co.uk/assessment

Copyright © Rising Stars UK Ltd 2016
First published in 2015 by Rising Stars UK Ltd, part of Hodder Education, an Hachette UK company, Carmelite House, 50 Victoria Embankment, London EC4Y 0DZ

Impression number   10 9 8
Year   2020 2019 2018 2017

All rights reserved. Apart from any use permitted under UK copyright law, no part of this publication may be reproduced or transmitted in any form or by any means, electronic or mechanical, including photocopying and recording, or held within any information storage and retrieval system, without permission in writing from the publisher. This publication is excluded from the reprographic licensing scheme administered by the Copyright Licensing Agency Ltd.

Typeset in India

Printed and bound by CPI Group (UK) Ltd, Croydon, CR0 4YY

A catalogue record for this title is available from the British Library

ISBN 978 1 471 80625 4

Contents

1 Introduction — 07
    Why use *PUMA*? — 07
    Measuring and following progress using *PUMA* — 09
    When to use each *PUMA* test — 10
    Mathematics demand progression in *PUMA* — 10
    Who can be assessed using *PUMA*? — 12

2 Administering the *PUMA* tests — 13
    When to test — 13
    Group size — 13
    Timing — 13
    Preparation — 13
    Administering the test — 13

3 Answers and mark schemes — 15
    Marking the answers — 15
    Finding the total raw score — 15
    Profiling performance by category — 15
    Making a visual record of progress — 15
    Obtaining other scores — 16
    Answers and mark schemes for each test — 17
    Record sheet for each test (photocopiable) — 51

4 Obtaining and interpreting test scores — 55
    Summative measures — 55
    Diagnostic and formative interpretation — 63
    Reporting progress with the Hodder Scale — 64
    Predicting future performance with the Hodder Scale — 67
    Case studies — 72

5	**Technical information**	**74**
	Standardisation sample	74
	Reliability	74
	Validity	77
6	**Standardised score tables**	**79**
	Standardised scores for *PUMA*	79
	Age-standardised scores for *PUMA*	84

Appendix A: Facilities for each question — **109**

Appendix B: Thresholds obtained algorithmically from facilities — **114**

Acknowledgements

A team effort led to the creation and development of the suite of *PUMA* tests:

- The author of the questions was Caroline Cooke.
- Lynda Nash advised on the questions and papers. Together with Carol MacIntosh and Tricia Highton, she also undertook the initial trials of them in St Martin at Shouldham Primary and Cheveley Primary respectively. Tom Daniel in Peafield Lane Primary and Hilary Southwell in Cotgrave Candleby Lane School undertook the second phase trials across these schools.
- Viv Kilburn was the language consultant.
- Jane Swift was the artist.
- Tony Kiek and Colin McCarty undertook the statistical analyses and produced the standardised scores and value-added predictions from the marks obtained in the trials in each of the four terms.
- Colin McCarty designed the suite of tests together with the predictive and diagnostic information for teachers. He managed all the stages of the development and standardisation. He worked closely with Chas Knight and then Emma Rees, the publishers at Hodder, to present tests, mark schemes and information in easy-to-use formats.

Our sincere thanks go to the staff of the following schools, who administered the testing for the standardisation, and the many thousands of pupils who took the assessments each term.

Annesley Primary School, Kirkby-in-Ashfield, NG17 9BW
Barham CE Primary School, Barham, CT4 6NX
Buckingham Primary School, Hull, HU8 8UG
Bywell CE Junior School, Dewsbury, WF12 7LX
Elveden Primary Academy, Elveden, IP24 3TN
Forest Academy, Brandon, IP27 0FP
High Ash CE Primary School, Great Brickhill, MK17 9AS
Kedington Primary Academy, Kedington, CB9 7QZ
King Richard School, Paulsgrove, PO6 4QP
Langley Park Primary School, Langley Park, DH7 9XN
Laureate Primary School, Newmarket, CB8 0AN
Little Hallingbury School, Little Hallingbury, CM22 7RE
Ludham Primary School, Ludham, NR29 5QN
Mapplewell Primary School, Staincross, S75 6BB
Marfleet Primary School, Hull, HU9 5RJ
Newton Poppleford Primary, Newton Poppleford, EX10 0EL
North Petherwin Primary School, Launceston, PL15 8NE
Old Hall Primary School, Bury, BL8 4LU
Our Lady and St. Oswald's RC Primary School, Oswestry, SY11 2TG
Pinkwell Primary School, Hayes, UB3 1PG
Redcastle Family School, Thetford, IP24 3PU
Roose Primary School, Barrow-In-Furness, LA13 0HF
Royal Hospital School, Ipswich, IP9 2RX
Southcoates Primary School, Hull, HU9 3TW
St Chad's RC Primary School, Manchester, M8 0SP
St Christopher's Primary School, Red Lodge, IP28 8XQ
St Dunstan's RC Primary School, Moston, M40 9HF
St Luke's CE Primary School, Tiptree, CO5 0SU
St Matthew's CE Primary School, Bradford, BD5 8HT
Swaythling Primary School, Southampton, SO17 3SZ
Sythwood School and Children's Centre, Woking, GU21 3AX
Warcop CE Primary School, Appleby, CA16 6NX
Whitchurch Primary School, Whitchurch, BS14 0PT
Windhill Primary School, Bishops Stortford, CM23 2NE
Woodstock CE Primary School, Woodstock, OX20 1LL
Worfield Primary School, Worfield, WV15 5LF

1 Introduction

Progress in Understanding Mathematics Assessment (*PUMA*) provides a standardised assessment of a pupil's mathematics attainment, plus a profile of mathematics skills, which helps you identify those pupils who may need further teaching and practice, as well as enabling you to celebrate success. *PUMA* is designed for whole-class use, with pupils of all abilities.

Written to the new National Curriculum, *PUMA* is designed to be used toward the end of each term in each primary school year in order to measure and monitor pupils' progress and to provide reliable, predictive and diagnostic information. Separate tests are available for the summer term in Reception and for each of the autumn, spring and summer terms in Years 1 to 6.

The tests are simple and quick to administer, and straightforward to mark. Each test takes between 30 and 60 minutes, depending on the year.

The tests provide thorough coverage of the new National Curriculum Programme of Study for each particular year. Curriculum Maps, breaking down the Programme of Study for the year into each term, are available on the Hodder Education website (www.hoddereducation.co.uk/puma/). All the schools taking part in the initial trialling and standardisation followed these Curriculum Maps, to ensure that the pupils were fully prepared for the tests and so that *PUMA* is a valid assessment of the new National Curriculum.

Why use *PUMA*?

Using *PUMA* provides many benefits to the teacher. First, *PUMA* gives reliable **summative information**, for example:

- *PUMA* uniquely provides three carefully designed tests for each year. This enables you to follow the progress of your pupils from term to term, as well as from year to year throughout primary school.
- Scores have been calibrated onto the Hodder Scale to allow you to see small increments of progress from term to term and to compare progress against national norms (see page 64).
- *PUMA* test scores help you to set appropriate and meaningful targets for your pupils and to monitor pupils' progress.
- The Department for Education wishes schools to be able to show the progress pupils make between Baseline, Key Stage 1 and Key Stage 2 stages of education. *PUMA* tests can provide you with an external reference for all intermediate stages, that is end of terms and end of years, so that you may report your value-added term by term, as well as monitoring to ensure pupils are on target.

PUMA also has a **diagnostic capability** and, therefore, allows you to investigate strengths and weaknesses of your pupils' mathematics skills. To enable you to use the information gained in this formative way, total scores on the tests can be broken down into distinct aspects of mathematics, thus giving a useful **profile** which reflects the categories of the new National Curriculum.

The categories used in *PUMA* are:

- number, place value and rounding
- addition, subtraction, multiplication and division, algebra
- fractions, decimals and percentages, ratio and proportion
- measures
- geometry: shapes position, direction, motion
- statistics and data handling.

PUMA systematically assesses pupils' mathematics skills and knowledge as shown in Table 1.1 below. The balance of the questions assessing these categories remains fairly constant as the tests become more demanding, helping you to pinpoint where pupils may be under-performing or making excellent progress.

The balance of marks displayed in Table 1.1 closely matches the new Key Stage 1 and 2 test profiles of coverage. In the Mathematics Test Frameworks, the Key Stage 1 and 2 profile of content domain is consistently: 65–75% for number (including ratio and proportion, and algebra at KS2); and 25–35% for measurement, geometry and statistics.

Table 1.1: Distribution of marks across the new National Curriculum

	Number		Overall geometry, measures and statistics	Geometry and measures	Statistics and data handling
	%	Approx. marks per test	%	Approx. marks per test	Approx. marks per test
PUMA R	65–70	20	25–35	10	–
PUMA 1	65–70	20	25–30	10	–
PUMA 2	65–70	20	25–30	8	2
PUMA 3	65–70	27	25–30	10	3
PUMA 4	65–70	27	25–30	10	3
PUMA 5	65–70	34	30–35	12	4
PUMA 6	65–70	34	30–35	12	4

You can also examine the performance of pupils on each question. The percentage of pupils that answered each question correctly in the national standardisation (that is, the facility value) enables you to easily compare the performance of your own pupils with those in the national sample.

PUMA will help you answer parents, governors, inspectors or headteachers who ask:

- How has *my* child done compared to others of his or her age or year group?
- What pattern of performance do pupils at a particular level achieve and how does my child (or class) compare to this?
- Has this pupil made good progress from year to year?
- What would be a reasonable level of achievement for this pupil next term?
- What are the strengths or successes of this pupil (or class)?

- What individual and class targets are appropriate and realistic?
- On what aspects of mathematics should this pupil focus to maximise progress?
- What would constitute good, average or poor progress for this pupil (or class)?

This manual contains all the information you need to obtain standardised scores, age-standardised scores, mathematics ages, a score on the Hodder Scale and a profile of performance on the various categories of questions. All together, the various scores provide a wealth of information that will support you in managing learning in your classroom.

PUMA Interactive and online reporting

Using *PUMA Interactive*, you can unlock even more diagnostic information. If you are using the pencil-and-paper tests, the online reporting tool on Rising Stars Assessment online will let you analyse group performance (for example, by class and/or gender), track pupil performance through the school and generate individual progress predictions. It also provides a fully interactive option so that your pupils can take the tests on-screen, in full colour. This is then automatically marked, analysed and individual and class reports made available.

Measuring and following progress using *PUMA*

PUMA provides a standardised assessment of a pupil's mathematics attainment. The following measures can be obtained from *PUMA*:

- a **standardised score** to place the pupils' scores on a standard scale for reporting
- an **age-standardised score** so that a pupil's score can be compared with others of the same age
- a **percentile** to give you a quick view about a pupil's score compared to the standardisation sample
- a **mathematics age** for a quick at-a-glance reference
- a score on the **Hodder Scale** for easy monitoring of pupils' progress
- a **points score**, widely used by local authorities for ranking schools.

The use of each of these scores is explained more fully in Chapter 4 *Obtaining and interpreting test scores*.

The *PUMA* test results have been statistically linked from term to term and year to year to show a clear set of information, enabling you to monitor strengths and weaknesses and track progress through the whole primary phase, while also enabling quite detailed comparisons of individual patterns of performance against the norms and patterns for the term or year.

Underpinning all this is the Hodder Scale which is a decimal scale. It enables you to monitor small increments of progress from term to term. The Hodder Scale acts as a common 'spine' on which all of the *PUMA* tests across the whole primary phase are plotted. (See Table 4.6 on page 68 which draws this all together.) It provides the statistical basis for *predicting* pupil progress and future attainment, based on the termly performance data of over 10 000 pupils nationally.

Profiling test scores

If you are using the paper test, you may complete the profile on the front cover of the pupil's test booklet. Codes alongside each mark in the test booklet allow you to collate the pupil's performance against assessment guidelines and build a picture of each pupil's performance that will let you follow progress, measure value-added and provide a set of validated data for comparison in future years.

The profile scores can also be plotted on the photocopiable Record Sheets (pages 51–54) so that you can view pupils' progress relative to national average performance for each aspect of mathematics.

If you wish, you can also average your pupils' scores to create an overall class profile. The pattern revealed may inform both teaching and target-setting as it will highlight the mathematics skills in which pupils are secure and those which need further work.

Alternatively, input the scores into Rising Stars Assessment online, for automatic profiling and reporting.

When to use each *PUMA* test

The test used at the end of the **autumn term** includes questions relating to the mathematics covered in earlier years. It should be used to baseline the pupils as they will have had only one term of teaching on this particular year's curriculum and are likely to be an unfamiliar class for the teacher.

The test used at the end of the **spring term** is a 'transitional' test containing some material from the previous year, but building on this with material from the current year to make it more difficult than the autumn test.

The test used at the end of the **summer term** is matched to the curriculum for the year as described in the new National Curriculum introduced by the Government for use from 2014. These summer tests are challenging, as required by the curriculum, but they assess only subject content that is expected to be taught during that particular year so that teachers may provide evidence to headteachers, governors, parents and Ofsted.

Mathematics demand progression in *PUMA*

Each test for each term has been carefully written to ensure there is a steady progression in the demand of the mathematics. Tables 1.2 and 1.3 show this progression in demand for the Key Stage 2 tests in terms of demand and National Standards, while Table 5.3 on page 78 shows the progression across the *PUMA* series.

To help teachers monitor the progress of their pupils from term to term and year to year, and to provide an effective way of describing and monitoring progress, we have matched *PUMA* results to our tried-and-tested Hodder Scale.

The full Hodder Scale is presented in Table 4.5. It runs from 0–6+, but for ease of reference, we have conflated the scale into three categories, to help describe the demand of the questions in *PUMA*:

- *low* covers the range 0.0–0.2 for each number on the scale (e.g. 1.0–1.2, 2.0–2.2, etc)
- *mid* covers the range 0.3–0.6 for each number on the scale
- *high* covers the range 0.7– 0.9 for each number on the scale.

We have called this conflated scale, the Hodder Scale of Demand and have labelled each question according to its demand in the mark schemes.

In October 2014, the Standards and Testing Agency published draft Performance Descriptors for Key Stage 1 and 2, to give teachers clear guidelines against which to measure pupils at the end of Years 2 and 6. We have categorised every *PUMA* question against the draft Performance Descriptors and present an overview of the coverage for each test in Table 1.2 below, illustrating the range of those tests. Together with Table 1.3 (showing the balance of demand indicated by the Hodder Scale), this information will help teachers select tests that may be more appropriate for weak or able pupils who would find the test for the particular term too hard or easy. We will review and update our question analysis and make this available, as appropriate, when the Performance Descriptors are finalised.

Table 1.2: Demand of mathematics in each *PUMA* test at Key Stage 2, showing the distribution of marks against the draft Performance Descriptors

	Performance descriptors					
	working towards KS1	emerging KS1	expected KS1	exceeding KS1, emerging KS2	expected KS2	exceeding KS2
Y3 Autumn	4	11	12	13		
Y3 Spring		5	16	18	1	
Y3 Summer		2	12	20	6	
Y4 Autumn	1	11	14	5	9	
Y4 Spring	1	2	7	14	16	
Y4 Summer		1	6	14	19	
Y5 Autumn				25	24	1
Y5 Spring				12	34	4
Y5 Summer				8	38	4
Y6 Autumn				13	27	10
Y6 Spring				11	30	9
Y6 Summer				3	36	11

Table 1.3: The design demand of mathematics in each *PUMA* test at Key Stage 2, showing the distribution of demand as matched to the Hodder Scale

	Hodder Scale reference of demand for KS2																
	Low 1	Mid 1	High 1	Low 2	Mid 2	High 2	Low 3	Mid 3	High 3	Low 4	Mid 4	High 4	Low 5	Mid 5	High 5	6	Total
PUMA 3 Autumn		1	2	8	6	3	3	6	9	1	1						40
PUMA 3 Spring				5	4	7	5	9	6	2	2						40
PUMA 3 Summer				3	4	4	11	9	5	2	2						40
PUMA 4 Autumn				4	4	6	7	4	5	6	4						40
PUMA 4 Spring					3	3	7	10	6	5	5	1					40
PUMA 4 Summer						2	13	6	5	3	9	2					40
PUMA 5 Autumn						5	6	9	7	3	8	7	5				50
PUMA 5 Spring							1	10	8	8	6	9	4	2	2		50
PUMA 5 Summer							5	5	3	9	6	7	5	5	5		50
PUMA 6 Autumn							6	9	6	7	5	5	2	4	3	3	50
PUMA 6 Spring							1	4	4	12	9	2	4	3	5	6	50
PUMA 6 Summer							2	3	2	5	6	12	6	6	1	7	50

Who can be assessed using *PUMA*?

The spread of demand of the tests shown in Tables 1.2 and 1.3 allows you to use each test with wide ability groups, including less and more able learners, and allows all pupils to experience some success.

Less able pupils may benefit from taking tests intended for earlier terms or years, where they are more likely to experience success and be able to demonstrate what they know and understand rather than struggling with skills and concepts that are too demanding for them.

In a similar way, able pupils following an accelerated pathway may take tests intended for older age groups.

Note, however, it may not be possible to obtain an age-standardised score or percentile if the pupil is outside the chronological age range of the age-standardised score table for the test used – although you will still be able to obtain a Hodder Scale score.

2 Administering the *PUMA* tests

When to test

The *PUMA* tests should ideally be used just before the end of term, as they have been designed to assess the National Curriculum objectives presented in the *PUMA* Curriculum Map for that term.

Since the standardisation tests were given in late November, March/April and late June, similar timings will produce the most dependable data; but, if the subject content has been taught, the timing is not critical.

Group size

You can administer the tests to whole classes or large groups if you feel comfortable doing so. However, with weaker Year 3 pupils it is likely to be better if carried out in small groups of perhaps five or six children of similar ability so that pauses could be taken if required, with teaching assistants also delivering the test.

Timing

A maximum time of **50 minutes** for the Year 3 and 4 tests and **60 minutes** for the Year 5 and 6 tests is advised.

In practice, informed by the standardisation trials, the test times are well under 1 minute per mark. Therefore, pupils should be able to complete the test in the time suggested unless they are particularly hesitant or slow workers where extra time may be allowed.

Preparation

Each pupil will need the appropriate test booklet plus a pencil or pen, an eraser and a ruler. No calculators or other equipment should be used.

Before the test, explain the following key points to pupils:

- Pupils should write their answers clearly. If they change their mind, they should cross out or rub out the wrong answer and write in the new answer.
- They may find some questions difficult. They should not worry about these questions, but should just try their best and then carry on.

Administering the test

Give each pupil a test booklet. Ask them to write their names on the front cover. The other information can be supplied by the teacher or teaching assistant when marking the test.

If any pupils are uncertain about what they have to do, you may give some additional explanation to help them understand the requirements of the test, but **do not** help with the mathematical content of the question.

If the results are to be reliable, it is important that the pupils work alone, without copying from each other or discussing their answers. Remind pupils of this if necessary.

3 Answers and mark schemes

Once the pupils have completed the test, their answers may be marked using the answers and mark schemes found in this chapter.

Marking the answers

- Mark boxes in the right-hand margins of each test booklet indicate where a mark can be gained.
- Some questions have more than one part, or attract more than 1 mark, so you should follow the mark scheme carefully, using your professional judgement if necessary. For example, accept mirror reversals of single digits but not reversals of two-digit numbers. Equally, any clear indication of the answer is acceptable irrespective of what was asked for, e.g. a tick or a circle.
- For scores to be valid, you should **not** award half marks.

Finding the total raw score

To help with marking and collating the data, page totals may be recorded at the bottom right corner of each page of the test booklet. Simply add up the ticks on a page and write the page total in each box. You can then sum the page scores to find the pupil's total raw score.

Profiling performance by category

The code letters shown for each mark box may be used to profile the pupil's performance by category. Total the number of correct answers the pupil has obtained in each coded category (i.e. num, ops, frac, geom, meas, stat) and make a note of these category scores in the boxes on the front cover of the test booklet. Questions that involve problem solving are indicated by the code PS and the number of questions answered correctly in this category can also be recorded on the front of the test booklet.

Making a visual record of progress

You may make a visual record of the pupil's progress by transferring the category scores to the photocopiable Record Sheet, in the form of a bar chart. The national averages are shown in black on each bar of the chart, so that you can compare a child or a class performance against these. The Record Sheets are on pages 51–54.

Following the mark scheme for each test, the *Analysis of performance by category* table allows you to analyse the pupils' performance by category compared to the national averages. This information is also shown visually on the bar chart on the Record Sheet.

Obtaining other scores

Refer to the appropriate tables in this manual to obtain the standardised score, age-standardised score, percentile, mathematics age and Hodder Scale score for each pupil. Or use the online reporting tool in Rising Stars Assessment online, when launched, to automate the whole score conversion process and to unlock *PUMA*'s full performance analysis, diagnostic and predictive potential.

Answers and mark scheme: PUMA 3 Autumn

No.	Answer	Reference	Hodder Scale of demand
1	8 strawberries	ops, PS	mid 1
2	Boy joined to the cylinder and girl to the triangular prism *Both required*	geom	mid 2
3	8 − 5 = 3 3 + 6 = 9 *Both required and no others for the mark*	ops	high 1
4	Any 4 small triangles shaded	frac	mid 2
5	(a) 40 (b) 30	num num	mid 2 high 2
6	27, 31, 55 *All three required and no others for the mark*	num	low 2
7	(a) 60 (b) 11	ops ops	low 2 mid 2
8	(a) France (b) Greece and Turkey (c) 25	stat stat stat, PS	low 2 high 1 low 2
9	14 children	ops, PS	high 2
10	(a) pencil and pad (b) 20p, 5p, 2p ticked *No mark for 10p, 10p, 5p, 2p*	meas, PS meas, PS	mid 2 low 2
11	14cm	meas	mid 3
12	*Cross on the pentagon in the 'hexagons' section only*	geom	high 2
13	203, 223, 230, 302, 320	num	mid 2
14	Any two identical numbers *Accept two zeros*	ops	low 2
15	83, 103 445, 145	num num	low 2 low 2
16	*Crosses on both parallelogram and right-angled triangle only*	geom	high 3

No.	Answer	Reference	Hodder Scale of demand
17	7 groups	ops, PS	mid 3
18	573	ops	low 3
19	740 and 46 only	num	mid 3
20	Square correctly completed within 2mm of correct vertex, even if ruler not used	geom	mid 3
21	4x8 → 6 20x3 → 36 12÷3 → 4 24÷4 → 32 → 60 8 *All three correct for 2 marks or two correct for 1 mark*	ops ops	low 3 mid 3
22	15 sweets	frac	high 3
23	(L-shape figure)	geom	mid 3
24	30	num, PS	low 3
25	845 + 1	ops	high 3
26	(a) 40 minutes (b) any 1 section shaded on the left-hand cake and any 2 sections shaded on the right-hand cake *Both required for the mark in (b)* *Vertical faces need not be shaded*	meas frac	high 3 high 3
27	60 120	frac frac	high 3 low 4
28	(number line 0 to 2 with marks at 1/2, 3/4, 1 1/2) *Both should be accurate enough to be unambiguous*	frac frac	high 3 high 3
29	118	ops	high 3
30	30cm *Accept 0.3m if unit altered*	meas, PS	mid 4

PUMA 3 Autumn: Analysis of performance by category

Category	Number of marks available	National average mark	National %
Number	8	4.6	58
Operations	12	6.4	53
Fractions	7	1.8	26
Measures	5	1.6	36
Geometry	5	1.8	36
Statistics	3	2.4	80
Total	40	18.5	46
Problem solving	8	4.3	54

Answers and mark scheme: PUMA 3 Spring

No.	Answer	Reference	Hodder Scale of demand
1	8 sweets	frac	low 2
2	18	ops	mid 2
3	83 36	num num	low 2 low 2
4	16 boys	ops, PS	mid 2
5	(a) 65p (b) 35p *Award the mark for (b) if the answers to (a) and (b) sum to £1*	meas meas, PS	mid 2 low 3
6	88	num	high 2
7	× − + *All three required*	ops	low 2
8		frac	high 2
9	60	num	mid 2
10	24 cubes	ops, PS	high 2
11	Any 6 squares shaded	frac	high 3
12	670g	num, PS	high 2
13	(a) 2 (b) 2	geom geom	high 2 mid 3
14	56, 24, 72	num	mid 3
15	$3\frac{3}{4}$ 5	frac frac	mid 3 mid 3
16	17 fish	ops, PS	high 3
17	(a) 205 (b) 1016	num num	low 2 high 2
18	423	ops	high 3
19	$\frac{2}{5}$	frac	high 3
20	$\frac{7}{10}$	frac	low 3

No.	Answer	Reference	Hodder Scale of demand
21	(trapezium shape) (hexagon shape)	geom, PS geom, PS	low 3 mid 3
22	$\frac{1}{5}$ $\frac{3}{5}$ $\frac{5}{5}$ $\frac{7}{5}$ *All four required in this order*	frac	high 2
23	(a) 15 more people (b) 27 *Only 27 ticked* (c) 3 buses	stat, PS stat, PS stat, PS	low 3 low 3 mid 3
24	794	ops	high 3
25	10:10 1:50	meas meas	mid 3 high 3
26	6 vertices	geom	mid 3
27	35 pencils	ops, PS	low 4
28	4 × 6 and 3 × 8 *Both required*	ops	mid 3
29	375g	meas	mid 4
30	592	ops	mid 4
31	7	frac, PS	low 4

PUMA 3 Spring: **Analysis of performance by category**

Category	Number of marks available	National average mark	National %
Number	8	5.3	67
Operations	10	4.2	42
Fractions	9	4.2	47
Measures	5	1.9	38
Geometry	5	2.2	44
Statistics	3	1.2	40
Total	40	19.3	48
Problem solving	12	5.1	42

Answers and mark scheme: *PUMA 3 Summer*

No.	Answer	Reference	Hodder Scale of demand
1	350 400	num num	low 2 low 2
2	6 plums 15 sweets	ops, PS ops, PS	high 2 low 3
3	one thousand, one hundred and twenty Accept eleven hundred and twenty Accept phonetic spellings	num	low 3
4	15 mins	meas, PS	high 2
5	345	num, PS	mid 2
6	16cm	meas, PS	mid 2
7	721 + 42 = 763 42 + 721 = 763 Accept either	ops	low 3
8	250ml	meas	low 3
9	D	geom	mid 2
10	1.3 2.0 or 2	frac frac	low 2 low 3
11	<table><tr><th>hat colour</th><th>scarf colour</th></tr><tr><td>blue</td><td>red</td></tr><tr><td>blue</td><td>green</td></tr><tr><td>green</td><td>red</td></tr><tr><td>green</td><td>blue</td></tr></table>*All four combinations in any order for 2 marks or any two different combinations from the list of four for 1 mark*	ops, PS ops, PS	mid 2 low 3
12	257 293 653 *All three correct for 2 marks or any two correct for 1 mark*	ops ops	high 2 low 3

No.	Answer	Reference	Hodder Scale of demand
13	All three acute angles ticked	geom	mid 3
14	7, 11 32, 27 1 mark for each row correct	ops ops	mid 3 low 3
15	$\frac{2}{4}$ $\frac{3}{6}$ Both ticked and no others	frac	low 3
16	40 17 180 All three correct for 2 marks or any two correct for 1 mark	num num	low 3 mid 3
17	2 right angles 4 right angles	geom geom	low 3 mid 3
18	(a) 40 cakes (b) 15 cakes (c) 150 cakes	stat, PS stat, PS stat, PS	high 2 mid 3 mid 3
19	$\frac{5}{8}$	frac	mid 3
20	51 + 73, 73 + 51, 71 + 53 or 53 + 71 Accept any one	ops, PS	high 3
21	$\frac{5}{9}$	frac	high 3
22	24 grapes	ops, PS	high 3
23	15:20	meas	mid 3
24	$\frac{1}{2}$	frac	high 3
25	827 692	ops, PS ops, PS	mid 4 mid 3

No.	Answer	Reference	Hodder Scale of demand
26	(T-shape drawing)	geom	high 3
27	9 squares	frac, PS	low 4
28	260	ops	low 4
29	Cara, Ben, Dina *Correct order required*	meas, PS	mid 4

PUMA 3 Summer: **Analysis of performance by category**

Category	Number of marks available	National average mark	National %
Number	6	4.1	69
Operations	14	6.4	46
Fractions	7	3.3	48
Measures	5	2.6	52
Geometry	5	2.6	52
Statistics	3	1.7	56
Total	40	20.7	52
Problem solving	16	7.5	47

Answers and mark scheme: PUMA 4 Autumn

No.	Answer	Reference	Hodder Scale of demand
1	20	ops	low 2
2	47p	meas	low 2
3	(a) D (b) C	geom geom	mid 2 high 2
4	(a) 25 children (b) 9 girls	ops ops, PS	low 2 mid 2
5	16mph	meas	high 2
6	Any 2 rectangles shaded	frac	high 2
7	250	num	mid 2
8	24, 48 Both required	num	mid 2
9	C, D Both required and no others	geom	low 3
10	60 cherries	ops, PS	high 2
11	<table><tr><th>rounds to 150</th><th>rounds to 160</th><th>rounds to 170</th></tr><tr><td>154</td><td>161 156</td><td>169 172</td></tr></table>All four numbers required	num	low 3
12	50 30 16 All three required	num	low 3
13	(a) Isosceles triangle and trapezium ticked, only. Both required and no others for the mark	geom	low 3
	(b) Trapezium Correct spelling not required Do not accept quadrilateral	geom	mid 4
14	20 minutes	meas	low 3
15	4	num	high 2
16	12 7 × 3 Both required Accept 3 × 7	num	high 2

No.	Answer	Reference	Hodder Scale of demand
17	(a) Ben and Sarah (b) £15 *Accept £15.00, but not £15.0* (c) £80 *Accept £80.00, but not £80.0*	stat stat, PS stat, PS	low 2 high 3 low 4
18	7.3 *Accept* $7\frac{3}{10}$	frac	mid 3
19	$3\frac{1}{3}$, $4\frac{2}{3}$ Both required	frac	low 3
20	< < >	ops ops ops	mid 3 mid 3 high 3
21	30 weeks	meas	high 3
22	522 10	ops frac	low 4 mid 3
23	$\frac{1}{4}$ — 0.25 $\frac{1}{2}$ — 0.5 $\frac{4}{10}$ — 0.4	frac frac	low 4 low 4
24	8 jugs	meas	high 3
25	15 eggs	frac	low 4
26	(8, 3)	geom	low 4
27	10 735 *Accept with or without space or comma*	num	low 3
28	958 or 938 *Accept either for the mark*	num, PS	high 3
29	(a) 9 flags (b) 8 flags	ops, PS ops, PS	mid 4 mid 4
30	8575	ops	mid 4

PUMA 4 Autumn: **Analysis of performance by category**

Category	Number of marks available	National average mark	National %
Number	8	5.0	63
Operations	11	4.9	44
Fractions	7	2.3	33
Measures	5	2.4	48
Geometry	6	2.5	42
Statistics	3	1.5	49
Total	40	18.7	47
Problem solving	7	2.4	34

Answers and mark scheme: PUMA 4 Spring

No.	Answer	Reference	Hodder Scale of demand
1	Accept any two different pairs which sum to 190, e.g. 80 and 110, 135 and 55, 1 and 189, 100 and 90	ops	mid 2
2	[diagram of arrow shape reflected across dashed horizontal line of symmetry]	geom	low 3
3	403 sweets	num	high 2
4	80 nuts	frac, PS	mid 2
5	18 fish	ops, PS	low 3
6	(a) 300 (b) 1350	num num	mid 2 high 2
7	(6,5)	geom, PS	mid 3
8	$2\frac{3}{4}$	frac	high 3
9	400, 500, 700 *Do not accept 400 and 600 with two ticks*	ops, PS	mid 3
10	(a) 3.5kg or $3\frac{1}{2}$ kg (b) 1.5kg or $1\frac{1}{2}$ kg (c) 3kg	stat, PS stat, PS stat, PS	low 3 high 3 mid 3
11	[four triangles matched to labels: right-angled, equilateral, isosceles, scalene]	geom	mid 3
12	3085 3853	num	high 2
13	260	ops	mid 3

No.	Answer	Reference	Hodder Scale of demand
14	<table><tr><th>right angles</th><th>acute angles</th><th>obtuse angles</th></tr><tr><td>1</td><td>2</td><td>1</td></tr></table> Both required	geom	high 3
15	66, 54, 18 All three and no others required for the mark	num	low 3
16	(a) 9 coins (b) £1.60	meas, PS meas, PS	low 3 low 3
17	8 packs	ops, PS	mid 3
18	561, 605, 599 All three and no others required for the mark	num	mid 3
19	Any 8 squares shaded	frac	low 4
20	7	ops, PS	mid 4
21	(a) £6.60 (b) £3.40 Award the mark for (b) if the answers for (a) and (b) sum to £10	frac, PS frac, PS	mid 3 high 3
22	127	ops	high 3
23	11, -1, -13 All three correct for 2 marks or any two correct for 1 mark	num num	low 3 mid 3
24	2 and 24 4 and 12 These pairs can be in any order within the list	ops ops	high 3 low 4
25	<table><tr><th>time</th><th>24-hour clock</th></tr><tr><td>20 minutes to 11 in the morning</td><td>10:40</td></tr><tr><td>25 past 4 in the afternoon</td><td>16:25</td></tr></table>	meas meas	low 4 mid 4
26	3500ml Answer must be in ml	meas	high 4
27	$\frac{3}{5}$	frac	mid 3
28	**3** squares down **5** squares to the right Both required	geom	mid 4
29	1548	ops	mid 4

No.	Answer		Reference	Hodder Scale of demand
30	number with **one** decimal place	nearest whole number	frac frac	low 4 low 4
	35.8	36		
	39.5–40.4 Accept any number within this range inclusive	40		
31	100		frac	mid 4

PUMA 4 Spring: **Analysis of performance by category**

Category	Number of marks available	National average mark	National %
Number	8	5.3	66
Operations	10	4.0	40
Fractions	9	3.4	38
Measures	5	1.7	34
Geometry	5	2.1	42
Statistics	3	1.7	56
Total	40	18.3	46
Problem solving	13	6.3	48

Answers and mark scheme: PUMA 4 Summer

No.	Answer	Reference	Hodder Scale of demand
1	CDAB	geom	low 3
2	 	×	2	9	12
5	10	45	60
6	12	54	72
3	6	27	36 | *Seven or eight correct for 2 marks; five or six correct for 1 mark*	ops ops	high 2 low 3
3	2182 cards	ops, PS	high 3
4	(ticks on the small upright triangle, the small inverted triangle, and the right-pointing triangle)	geom	low 3
5	9273	num	low 3
6	(a) 8752 (b) 128	num num, PS	high 2 mid 4
7	−5°C, −3°C, 0°C, 3°C, 5°C	num	mid 3
8	C	meas	low 3
9	14 56	num num	low 3 low 3
10	500	ops	mid 3
11	0.33	frac	low 3
12	*1 mark for the additions and 1 mark for the multiplications* 50+50+50+50+50 → 250 70 × 4 → 280 60+60+60+60 → 240 3 × 90 → 270	ops ops	mid 3 low 3
13	(a) Cara (b) Dani	meas, PS meas, PS	high 3 low 3
14	£5.33	frac, PS	high 3

No.	Answer	Reference	Hodder Scale of demand
15	$\frac{14}{8}$ or $1\frac{6}{8}$ or $1\frac{3}{4}$ Accept any of these	frac	mid 4
16	90 eggs	ops, PS	mid 4
17	(3,5) and (2,4) Both required and no others for the mark	geom, PS	low 4
18	16 marbles	frac, PS	mid 4
19	9.85 5.89 Both required	frac	low 3
20	(a) 9 children	stat, PS	low 3
	(b) 5 children	stat, PS	mid 3
	(c) [smiley face and half smiley face]	stat, PS	low 3
21	53	ops	mid 4
22	Both D and B required for 1 mark Both C and E required for 1 mark | D | A B | C | E |	geom, PS geom, PS	high 4 low 4
23	LXIV Accept 64	num	mid 4
24	3000	num	mid 3
25	| fraction | decimal | | $\frac{3}{10}$ | 0.3 | | $\frac{57}{100}$ | **0.57** | | $\frac{7}{100}$ | 0.07 |	frac frac frac	mid 3 high 3 low 4
26	450	ops, PS	high 3
27	8cm	meas, PS	mid 4
28	BADC	meas	mid 4
29	$\frac{4}{6}$ $\frac{6}{9}$ Accept in either order	frac frac, PS	mid 4 high 4

Answers and mark scheme: *PUMA 4 Summer*

PUMA 4 Summer: Analysis of performance by category

Category	Number of marks available	National average mark	National %
Number	8	4.8	60
Operations	9	4.8	53
Fractions	10	4.7	47
Measures	5	2.5	49
Geometry	5	2.3	45
Statistics	3	2.2	72
Total	40	21.2	53
Problem solving	16	6.6	41

Answers and mark scheme: *PUMA 4 Summer*

Answers and mark scheme: PUMA 5 Autumn

No.	Answer	Reference	Hodder Scale of demand
1	35 pebbles	ops	high 2
2	Any 4 rectangles shaded	frac	mid 3
3	(a) 7 children (b) 22 children	stat, PS stat, PS	high 2 high 2
4	$2\frac{3}{4}$ and $1\frac{1}{4}$ $2\frac{1}{4}$ and $1\frac{3}{4}$ Accept either	frac	mid 4
5	(mirror line diagram with reflected triangles)	geom	low 3
6	(a) 70 (b) Any one of 32, 33 or 34	num num	high 2 low 3
7	52 sweets	ops, PS	low 3
8	4.5cm² or $4\frac{1}{2}$ cm²	meas	low 4
9	1.1, 2.1 Both required	frac	low 3
10	456 → 401 to 600; 192 → 0 to 200; 758 → 601 to 800; 902 → over 800; 89 → 0 to 200 All four required	num	mid 3

No.	Answer	Reference	Hodder Scale of demand
11	$\frac{3}{8}$	frac	mid 3
12	(a) £3.54 (b) £6.46 (c) 8 Accept follow through, i.e. if the answers to (a) and (b) add up to £10	meas meas, PS meas, PS	high 3 low 4 mid 3
13	717	ops	high 3
14	(a) 764 (b) 647 or 627	num, PS num, PS	high 2 low 3
15	1, 2, 3, 5, 6, 10, 15, 30 All required for the mark Do not penalise incorrect ordering as the instruction to put them in increasing order is only there to assist marking	ops	mid 4
16	(a) 3 (b) 50	ops ops	high 3 low 4
17	(a) 6 edges (b) 8 faces (c) 12 vertices	geom geom geom	high 3 high 4 high 4
18	(a) 20 more players (b) 75 players (c) can't tell	stat, PS stat, PS stat	low 3 high 3 mid 3
19	4336 members	ops, PS	high 4
20	(a) 60 (b) 90 (c) 40	frac frac frac	mid 3 high 4 low 5
21	592	num	high 3
22	5 cups	meas	mid 3
23	1 hr 40 mins	meas	high 4
24	<table><tr><td>×</td><td>8</td><td>3</td><td>4</td></tr><tr><td>9</td><td>72</td><td>27</td><td>36</td></tr><tr><td>3</td><td>24</td><td>9</td><td>12</td></tr><tr><td>6</td><td>48</td><td>18</td><td>24</td></tr></table> Eight or nine correct for 2 marks; six or seven correct for 1 mark	ops ops	mid 3 high 3
25	1 mark for *both* nearest 100, i.e. 36 300 and 79 800 1 mark for *both* nearest 1000, i.e. 36 000 and 80 000 Accept with or without commas and spaces	num num	mid 4 high 4
26	(a) 100 (b) 7500	ops ops	mid 4 mid 4

No.	Answer	Reference	Hodder Scale of demand
27	$\frac{2}{100}$ — 0.02 $\frac{1}{2}$ — 0.5 $\frac{2}{5}$ — 0.4	frac frac	mid 3 low 5
28	(a) A and C *only* (b) C and E *only*	geom geom	mid 4 low 5
29	23 *and* 29 Both required and no others for the mark	ops	high 4
30	(a) < (b) >	frac frac	mid 4 mid 4
31	a = 3cm b = 7cm Both required	meas	low 5
32	7656	ops	low 5

PUMA 5 Autumn: Analysis of performance by category

Category	Number of marks available	National average mark	National %
Number	8	4.3	54
Operations	13	5.0	39
Fractions	11	4.0	36
Measures	7	2.3	33
Geometry	6	2.0	33
Statistics	5	3.1	63
Total	*50*	*20.7*	*41*
Problem solving	10	5.5	55

Answers and mark scheme: 5 PUMA Spring

No.	Answer	Reference	Hodder Scale of demand
1	120°	geom	mid 3
2	4	num, PS	high 3
3	3700 1000	ops ops	mid 3 mid 3
4	$\frac{2}{4}$ and $\frac{3}{6}$ Both required and no others for the mark	frac	mid 3
5	24 hundreds 240 tens Both required and no others for the mark	num	high 3
6	4000 5000 Both required	ops, PS	low 4
7	Any two of $\frac{5}{4}$ $\frac{8}{3}$ $\frac{5}{2}$ ticked	frac	mid 3
8	(a) 2 009 909 (b) 290 099	num num	low 3 high 3
9	acute angle: d obtuse angle: c e All three required	geom	mid 3
10	18cm^3	meas	mid 3
11	362	ops	low 4
12	427 bees	ops, PS	low 4
13	3800	num, PS	mid 3
14	Arrow drawn at −8°C	num	high 3
15	12	ops, PS	high 3
16	2508	ops	high 3
17	406 500	num	high 3
18	9 5 [1] − 6 [6] 4 2 8 7 Allow carrying figures in the answer boxes provided they are clearly carrying figures, i.e. do not accept 11 in the top box	ops, PS ops, PS	mid 4 high 4

No.	Answer	Reference	Hodder Scale of demand
19	1.1 m	meas	low 4
20	 > < All three correct for 2 marks or any two correct for 1 mark	ops ops ops	low 4 mid 4
21	(a) £13.50 (b) 4:05pm Do not accept 4:5	meas, PS meas, PS	mid 3 mid 4
22	$\frac{5}{2}$ $\frac{7}{4}$ $3\frac{4}{5}$	frac frac	mid 4 high 4
23	3 537 000 577 300 Both required	num	mid 3
24	80%	frac	low 4
25	106	ops	high 4
26	43°	geom	mid 4
27	$\frac{4}{10} + \frac{4}{100}$ $\frac{44}{100}$ $\frac{440}{1000}$ All three correct and no others ticked for 2 marks Any two correct (and up to one wrong) for 1 mark	frac frac	high 3 low 5
28	2.5 3.1 Both required	frac	high 4
29	(a) 8 355 000 (b) 6 035 350	num num	low 4 high 4
30	10p	frac, PS	high 4
31	<table><tr><th></th><th>true for all rectangles</th><th>only true for squares</th><th>not true for any rectangles</th></tr><tr><td>all sides are the same length</td><td></td><td>✓</td><td></td></tr><tr><td>angles add up to 180°</td><td></td><td></td><td>✓</td></tr><tr><td>diagonals cross at right angles</td><td></td><td>✓</td><td></td></tr></table> All three correct for 2 marks or any two correct for 1 mark	geom, PS geom, PS	low 4 mid 5
32	405 Do not accept 4 5 without the zero place holder	ops	high 4
33	(a) 43mph or 44mph (b) 48km/h	stat stat	low 5 high 5

No.	Answer	Reference	Hodder Scale of demand
34	32.55	frac	high 4
35	(a) 36cm² (b) 6cm *Accept the square root of the answer to (a)*	meas meas, PS	mid 4 high 5
36	(7,1)	geom, PS	mid 5
37	4.06, 4.45, 4.5, 4.56, 4.6	frac	low 5
38	(a) 26 mins (b) 11:23	stat, PS stat, PS	high 4 low 5

PUMA 5 Spring: **Analysis of performance by category**

Category	Number of marks available	National average mark	National %
Number	10	5.6	56
Operations	13	5.7	44
Fractions	11	4.4	40
Measures	6	2.6	43
Geometry	6	2.4	41
Statistics	4	1.1	27
Total	50	21.7	44
Problem solving	16	6.0	38

Answers and mark scheme: PUMA 5 Summer

No.	Answer	Reference	Hodder Scale of demand
1	24, 48, 96 All three and no others required for the mark	ops	low 3
2	−4 14	num num	low 3 low 3
3	a e b All three correct for 2 marks or any two correct for 1 mark	geom geom	mid 3 high 4
4	16 000 sheets	ops, PS	mid 3
5	$\frac{3}{14}$	frac	low 4
6	405 000	num	low 3
7	$1\frac{1}{3}$ $-\frac{2}{3}$	frac frac	mid 3 mid 3
8	Asif Mina Both required	meas, PS	mid 4
9	150g	meas, PS	mid 3
10	1:30pm 15 minutes 3.5km or $3\frac{1}{2}$ km 45 minutes	stats, PS stats, PS stats, PS stats, PS	low 3 mid 4 high 3 high 4
11	0.3, 0.8, 0.9 All three and no others required for the mark	frac, PS	high 3
12	£6	ops, PS	low 4
13	4	ops	high 4
14	52 pages	ops, PS	high 3
15	*[diagram of cubes with circles marked on two faces]* Both circles on the correct faces for the mark	geom	low 4

No.	Answer	Reference	Hodder Scale of demand
16	50 400	ops	low 4
17	2, 3, 12	ops	low 4
18	65 girls and 55 boys Both required	ops, PS	high 4
19	1397	num, PS	high 5
20	2 30	ops ops	low 4 mid 4
21	$\frac{3}{8}$ $\frac{1}{2}$ $\frac{5}{8}$ $\frac{3}{4}$	frac	high 4
22	180	ops	low 4
23		geom, PS geom, PS	low 4 low 4
24	£28	frac, PS	low 5
25	150m²	meas, PS	high 4
26	188 packs	ops, PS	mid 5
27	4 whole pizzas	frac, PS	high 4
28	Accept any whole number between 245 000 and 249 999	num, PS	low 5
29	35%	frac, PS	mid 5
30	30cm	meas, PS	low 5
31	0.345, 0.4, 0.45, 0.5, 0.53	frac	low 5
32	(a) 8760 (b) 11 388 *Accept an answer for (b) that is 2628 (i.e. 438 x 6) larger than the answer produced for (a)*	ops ops	mid 4 high 5
33	2, 3	ops	high 5
34	0.055 505	frac frac	mid 4 mid 4
35	135°	geom, PS	mid 5
36	36, 64 Both required	num, PS	mid 5
37	27	ops	mid 5
38	50g 800g 8.95kg *Accept 8.950kg* All three correct for 2 marks or any two correct for 1 mark	meas meas	low 5 high 5
39	$\frac{7}{10}$	frac	high 5

PUMA 5 Summer: Analysis of performance by category

Category	Number of marks available	National average mark	National %
Number	6	2.7	45
Operations	16	6.1	39
Fractions	12	4.5	37
Measures	6	1.8	31
Geometry	6	2.7	44
Statistics	4	1.9	47
Total	*50*	*19.7*	*39*
Problem solving	23	7.9	34

Answers and mark scheme: PUMA 6 Autumn

No.	Answer	Reference	Hodder Scale of demand
1	1052 1152 *Both required*	num	low 3
2	$4\frac{3}{4}$ and $5\frac{1}{4}$ *Both required*	frac	low 3
3	(a) 22 cakes (b) 90 cakes	ops, PS frac	low 3 mid 3
4	Rectangle and both triangles ticked *only*	geom	mid 3
5	£3.75 Accept £3.75p, £3-75, £3-75p Do not accept £375 or £375p	meas	mid 3
6	95km/h Accept 94–96kmph	meas	low 3
7	819	ops	mid 3
8	9, 32 Both required 15, 45 Both required	ops ops, PS	low 3 mid 3
9	Arrow must be positioned closer to the middle, i.e. 2500, than to either 2000 or 3000 Accept answers in the range 2250 to 2750	num	mid 3
10	$\frac{3}{4}$, 0.52, 55% All three required and no others for the mark	frac	high 3
11			number of edges	number of faces	number of vertices
cube	12	6	8
triangular prism	9	5	6
square-based pyramid	8	5	5 | All correct for 2 marks or any two rows correct for 1 mark	geom geom	low 4 high 4
12	164g, 159g *Both required and no others for the mark*	num	low 4

No.	Answer	Reference	Hodder Scale of demand
13	<table><tr><td>×</td><td>12</td><td>9</td><td>7</td></tr><tr><td>8</td><td>96</td><td>72</td><td>56</td></tr><tr><td>11</td><td>132</td><td>99</td><td>77</td></tr><tr><td>6</td><td>72</td><td>54</td><td>42</td></tr></table> *Seven or eight correct for 2 marks; five or six correct for 1 mark*	ops ops	low 3 high 3
14	22cm	ops	mid 3
15	(a) Range 85–86cm (b) Range 45–46 months (c) Range 2–3cm (d) Range 16.5–17.5cm	stat stat, PS stat, PS stat, PS	high 3 mid 4 mid 4 6
16	12 020	ops	mid 3
17	8 weeks	ops	mid 4
18	(a) $\frac{3}{10}$ (b) $\frac{1}{3}$	frac frac	low 4 mid 5
19	<table><tr><th>kilograms</th><th>grams</th></tr><tr><td>5kg</td><td>5000g</td></tr><tr><td>2.4kg</td><td>**2400g**</td></tr><tr><td>$\frac{1}{2}$ kg</td><td>**500g**</td></tr><tr><td>**12.5kg or 12$\frac{1}{2}$ kg**</td><td>12 500g</td></tr></table> *All three correct for 2 marks or any two correct for 1 mark*	meas meas	mid 3 low 4
20	(a) £128 (b) 30 people	ops, PS ops, PS	low 4 high 4
21	400 000, 600 000 *Both required and no others for the mark*	num	low 4
22	Tom	frac, PS	mid 4
23	253	ops	mid 4
24	$6\frac{1}{8}$ $6\frac{1}{4}$ $6\frac{1}{2}$ $6\frac{5}{8}$ $6\frac{3}{4}$ *All required in this order*	frac	high 4
25	(a) 3000 (b) 60	num num	high 3 low 4
26	1, 2, 3, 6 *only* *Ignore the omission of 1*	ops	mid 5
27	(a) 54cm^2 (b) 48cm	meas meas	high 5 high 4

Answers and mark scheme: *PUMA 6 Autumn*

No.	Answer	Reference	Hodder Scale of demand
28			always	sometimes	never
multiples of 7 are even ...		✓	
prime numbers have exactly two factors ...	✓		
square numbers have an odd number of factors ...		✓	| *All three correct for 2 marks or any two correct for 1 mark*	ops, PS ops, PS	high 3 6
29	590 1000 0.59 *All three correct for 2 marks or any two correct for 1 mark*	frac frac	high 3 high 4
30	Dot in top vertex	geom, PS	mid 5
31	16	frac	low 5
32	28cm	meas, PS	mid 5
33	(8,10)	geom, PS	high 5
34	(a) 76 300 (b) 88 508 Accept answer for (b) if it is 12 208 (i.e. 8 x 1526) greater than the answer for (a)	ops ops	low 5 high 5
35	999 940	num, PS	6

PUMA 6 Autumn: **Analysis of performance by category**

Category	Number of marks available	National average mark	National %
Number	7	3.8	54
Operations	17	8.7	51
Fractions	10	4.3	43
Measures	7	3.0	43
Geometry	5	1.7	34
Statistics	4	1.5	38
Total	50	23.0	46
Problem solving	14	3.8	28

Answers and mark scheme: PUMA 6 Spring

No.	Answer	Reference	Hodder Scale of demand
1	63 710	ops	mid 3
2	$\frac{1}{2}$ — 50%, $\frac{1}{4}$ — 25%, $\frac{1}{10}$ — 10%, $\frac{1}{5}$ — 20%	frac	low 3
3	25 000	num	mid 3
4	72 000	ops	mid 3
5	$\frac{1}{7}$	frac, PS	high 3
6	2.7, 3.2, 4.1 All three required and no others for the mark	frac, PS	mid 4
7	5 faces, 5 vertices, 8 edges All three required	geom	mid 4
8	349	num, PS	mid 4
9	72, 4.5, 2.25 or equivalents All three correct for 2 marks or any two correct for 1 mark	num num	high 3 low 4
10	Kite	geom	mid 4
11	$\frac{1}{3}$	frac	low 4
12	520 350	num	low 4
13	7 × 7	ops	mid 3
14	2, 4, 8 All three required and no others for the mark	ops	low 4
15	3751 + 4523 1 mark for the top row and 1 mark for the second row	ops, PS ops, PS	high 3 low 4
16	4cm 26cm	meas, PS meas, PS	high 4 mid 5
17	250 × 100, 2500 × 10 Both required	num	high 3
18	(a) 15 (b) 20	frac frac	low 4 low 4
19	8 reams	ops, PS	mid 4

No.	Answer	Reference	Hodder Scale of demand
20	A, C Both required	geom, PS	mid 4
21	£300 000 £256 000 £299 999 All three required and no others for the mark	num	low 4
22	2.4	frac	low 4
23	(a) 13 800 vouchers (b) 6200 vouchers Award the mark if answers to (a) and (b) sum to 20 000	ops, PS ops, PS	low 4 high 4
24	(a) 700g (b) 60p	frac, PS frac, PS	mid 4 low 5
25	21 57	ops ops	low 4 high 5
26	£63.25	frac	mid 5
27	(−6,2)	geom	mid 4
28	(a) 2.175 litres Do not accept 2 litres 175 ml or 2175ml (b) 5 glasses	meas, PS meas, PS	high 5 mid 5
29	6kg	frac, PS	high 5
30	(a) £6 (b) £4.50	stat, PS stat	low 5 high 5
31	9 litres	frac, PS	high 5
32	$a = 42°$ $b = 21°$	geom geom, PS	mid 4 6
33	300cm²	meas	6
34	(a) 25% (b) £15	stat stat, PS	low 4 low 5
35	$\frac{5}{8}$	frac	6
36	(a) 25 squares (b) 24 (c) $s = 4n + 1$ Accept $4 × n + 1$ or $1 + 4 × n$ Do not accept words	ops ops, PS ops	low 5 6 6
37	9cm	meas	6

PUMA 6 Spring: Analysis of performance by category

Category	Number of marks available	National average mark	National %
Number	7	5.1	72
Operations	14	8.2	59
Fractions	13	7.2	55
Measures	6	1.8	31
Geometry	6	3.2	54
Statistics	4	1.8	46
Total	*50*	*27.3*	*55*
Problem solving	21	10.0	47

Answers and mark scheme: PUMA 6 Summer

No.	Answer	Reference	Hodder Scale of demand
1	48 8 72 42 9 5 *Five or six correct for 2 marks; three or four correct for 1 mark*	ops ops	low 3 mid 3
2	£10 000	ops, PS	mid 3
3	(a) 12 vertices (b) 18 edges	geom geom	mid 4 high 4
4	12cm	geom	high 4
5	(a) 10m (b) 7m	frac, PS frac, PS	low 4 mid 4
6	30°C	num	high 3
7	$\frac{1}{2}$ minute 40 seconds 3 hours 200 minutes *All required in this order*	meas	low 4
8	5 laps	meas, PS	mid 4
9	26 824	ops	low 4
10	(a) 7.86m (b) 6.5m *Do not accept 6.50*	frac frac	low 4 high 4
11	(a) 30, 35 *Both required* (b) 25 (c) B	stat, PS stat, PS stat, PS	low 3 high 3 mid 3
12		frac frac	mid 4 high 4

fraction	division	decimal
$\frac{1}{2}$	1 ÷ 2	0.5
$\frac{3}{4}$	3 ÷ 4	**0.75**
$\frac{2}{5}$	**2 ÷ 5**	**0.4**

All three correct for 2 marks or any two correct for 1 mark
Accept 0.40

No.	Answer	Reference	Hodder Scale of demand
13	70%	frac, PS	low 4
14	12 000 eggs	ops PS	low 5
15	60, 180 *Both required and no others for the mark*	ops	high 4

No.	Answer	Reference	Hodder Scale of demand
16	90° 18°	stat, PS frac, PS	mid 4 high 4
17	(a) 100 000 (b) 36 000	ops ops	high 4 low 5
18	(a) m + n = 19 or n + m = 19 or 19 = m + n *Do not accept words e.g. m plus n equals 19* (b) m = 16, n = 3 *Both required*	ops ops, PS	high 4 mid 5
19	60cm	frac, PS	high 4
20	(a) 120° (b) g = 180 – f	geom geom	mid 5 high 4
21	<table><tr><th>A < 16</th><th>B > 9</th><th>A – B</th></tr><tr><td>15</td><td>12</td><td>3</td></tr><tr><td>14</td><td>11</td><td>3</td></tr><tr><td>13</td><td>10</td><td>3</td></tr></table>*Rows may be in either order*	ops, PS	low 5
22	(a) 5, 6 *Both required* (b) $\frac{11}{15}$	frac frac	mid 4 mid 5
23	(a) 80km (b) 1 hr 15 mins	meas meas, PS	high 5 6
24	$\frac{6}{4} \frac{8}{5} \frac{5}{3} \frac{11}{6}$ *All required*	frac	6
25	(a) 30cm (b) 36cm	meas, PS meas, PS	low 5 6
26	<table><tr><th>number</th><th>rounded to the nearest 100</th><th>rounded to the nearest 1000</th></tr><tr><td>48 649</td><td>**48 600**</td><td>**49 000**</td></tr><tr><td>**range** **17 450–17 499**</td><td>17 500</td><td>17 000</td></tr></table>*1 mark for both numbers on top row, 1 mark for bottom row*	num num, PS	high 4 low 5
27	$\frac{3}{8}$	frac	low 5
28	(a) 96 000 (b) 96 768 *Accept an answer for (b) that is the answer to (a) + 768 (i.e. 32 x 24)*	ops ops	high 4 mid 5

No.	Answer	Reference	Hodder Scale of demand
29	450 × 100 Accept 45 000 65 thousand Accept 65 000 $\frac{1}{4}$ million Accept 250 000 30 × 10 000 Accept 300 000	num	mid 5
30	324	ops	mid 5
31	$2\frac{5}{6}$ Do not accept an improper fraction	frac	6
32	920 000	ops	6
33	$\frac{1}{6}$ Accept $\frac{2}{12}$	frac	6
34	(−4, −8)	geom	6

PUMA 6 Summer: **Analysis of performance by category**

Category	Number of marks available	National average mark	National %
Number	4	3.3	83
Operations	15	6.9	46
Fractions	15	5.8	39
Measures	6	2.2	37
Geometry	6	2.5	41
Statistics	4	3.2	81
Total	50	23.9	48
Problem solving	18	9.4	52

puma

Record Sheet

Pupil name ....

PUMA 3 Autumn

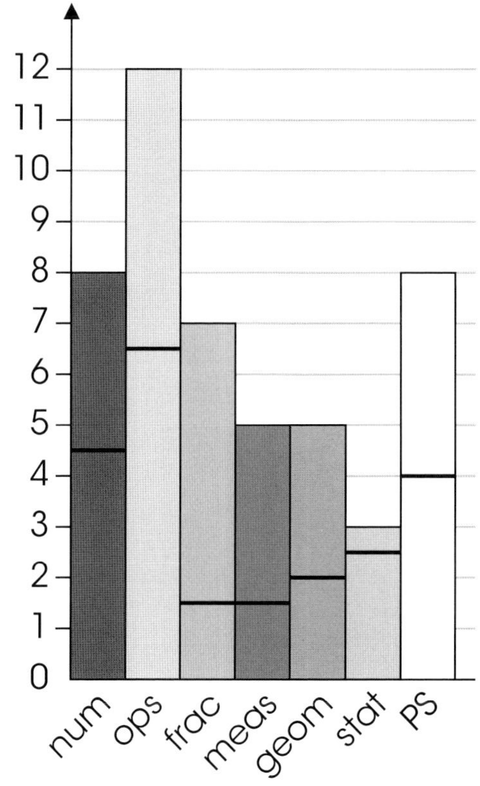

PUMA 3 Spring

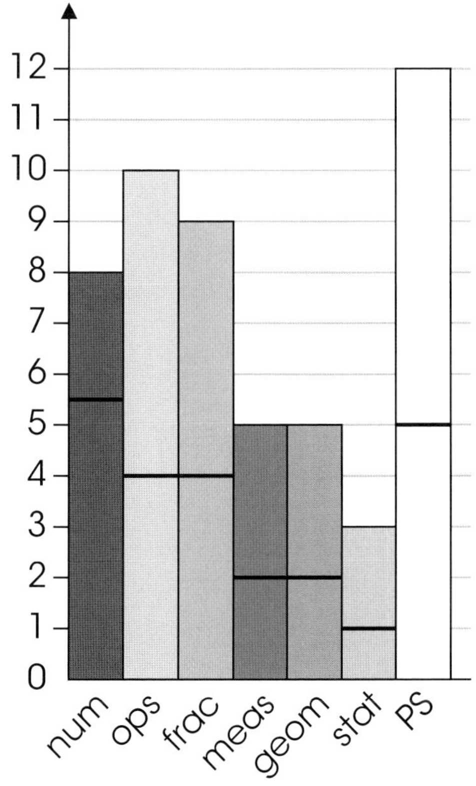

PUMA 3 Summer

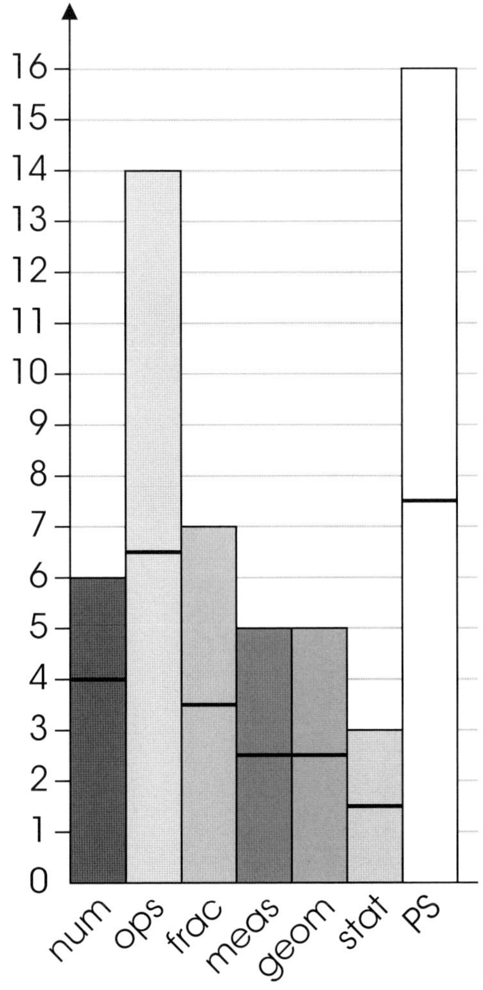

Raw Score _____ Hodder Scale _____ Raw Score _____ Hodder Scale _____ Raw Score _____ Hodder Scale _____

Photocopiable resource: this record sheet may be photocopied within the purchasing institution. Copyright © Hodder & Stoughton 2015.

puma Record Sheet

Pupil name ....

PUMA 4 Autumn

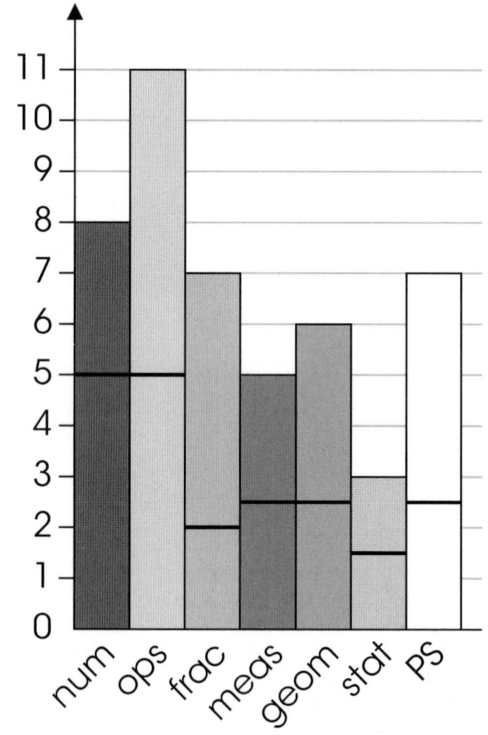

PUMA 4 Spring

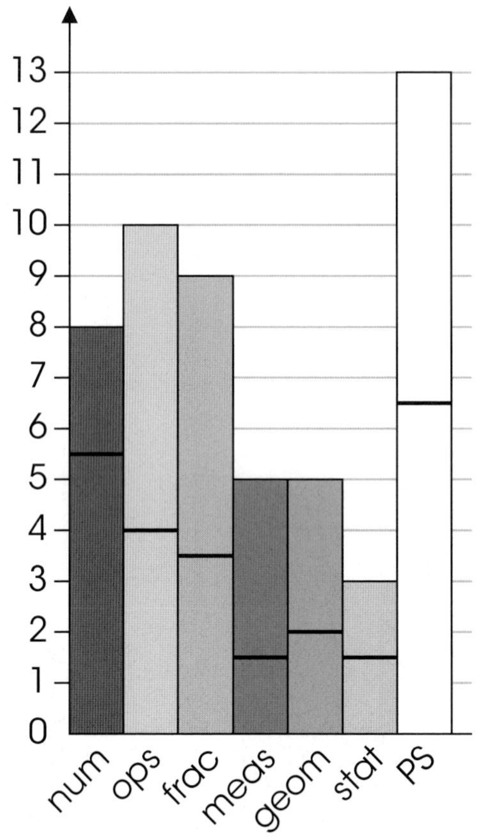

PUMA 4 Summer

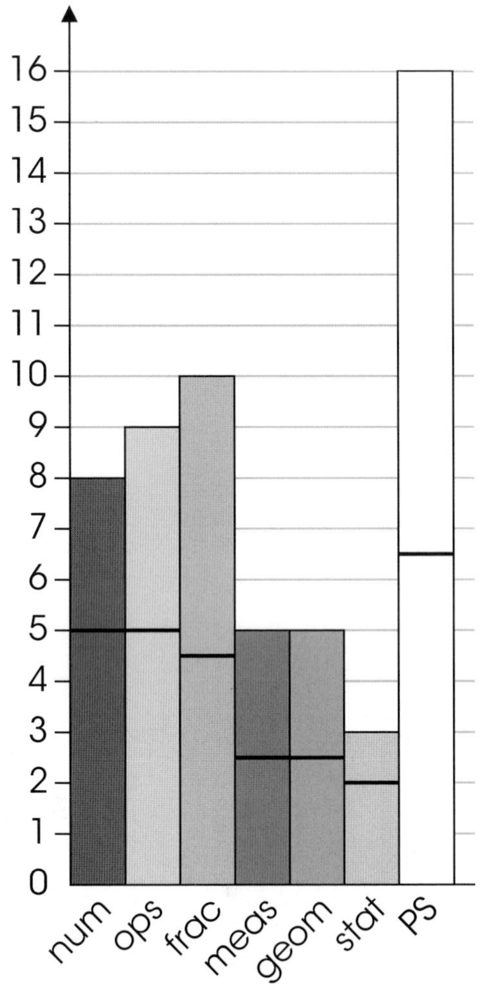

Raw Score _____ Hodder Scale _____ Raw Score _____ Hodder Scale _____ Raw Score _____ Hodder Scale _____

Photocopiable resource: this record sheet may be photocopied within the purchasing institution. Copyright © Hodder & Stoughton 2015.

puma Record Sheet

Pupil name ....

PUMA 5 Autumn

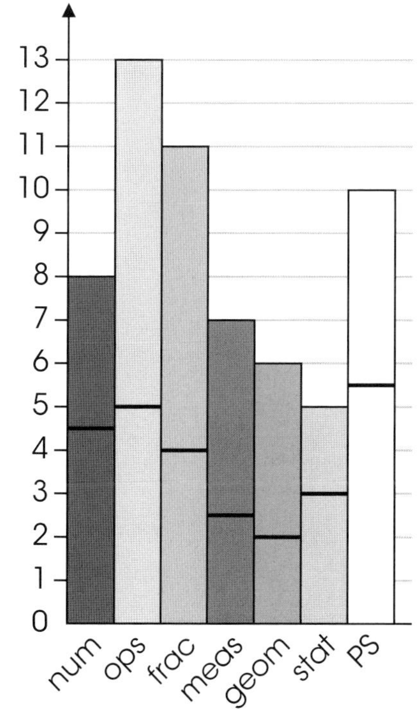

PUMA 5 Spring

PUMA 5 Summer

Raw Score _____ Hodder Scale _____ Raw Score _____ Hodder Scale _____ Raw Score _____ Hodder Scale _____

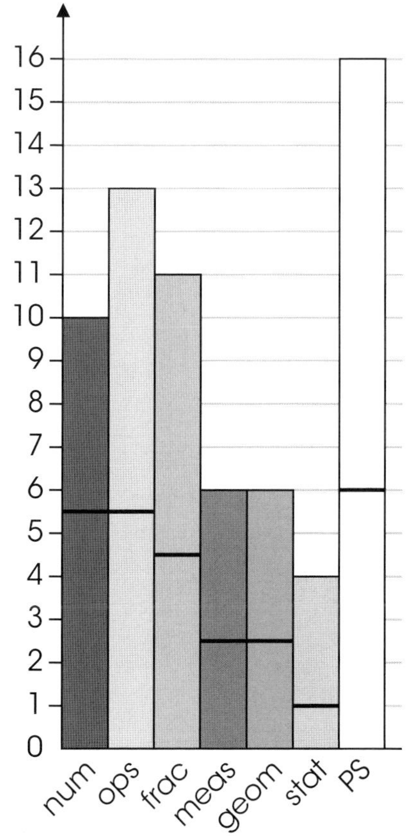

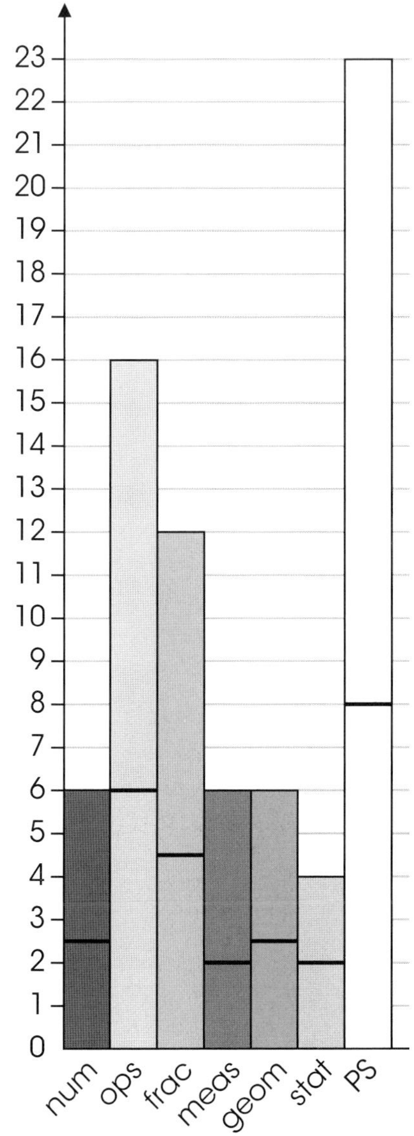

Photocopiable resource: this record sheet may be photocopied within the purchasing institution. Copyright © Hodder & Stoughton 2015

Record Sheet 53

puma Record Sheet

Pupil name ....

....

PUMA 6 Autumn

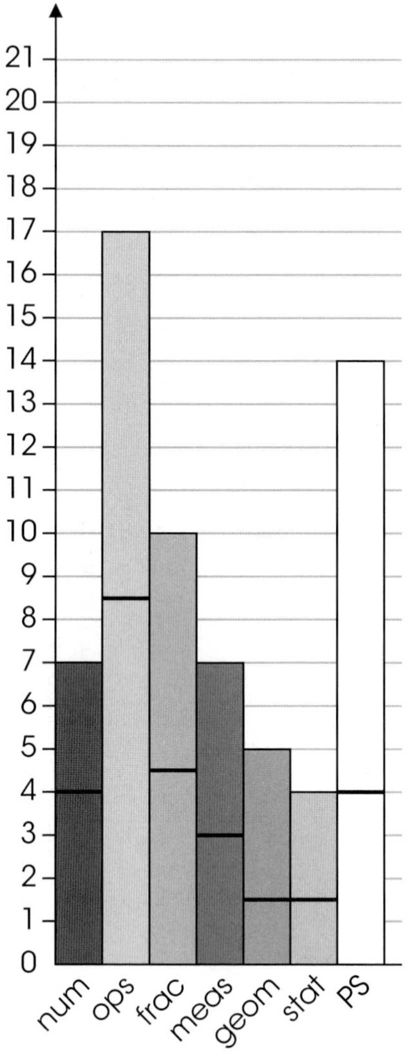

PUMA 6 Spring

PUMA 6 Summer

Raw Score _____ Hodder Scale _____ Raw Score _____ Hodder Scale _____ Raw Score _____ Hodder Scale _____

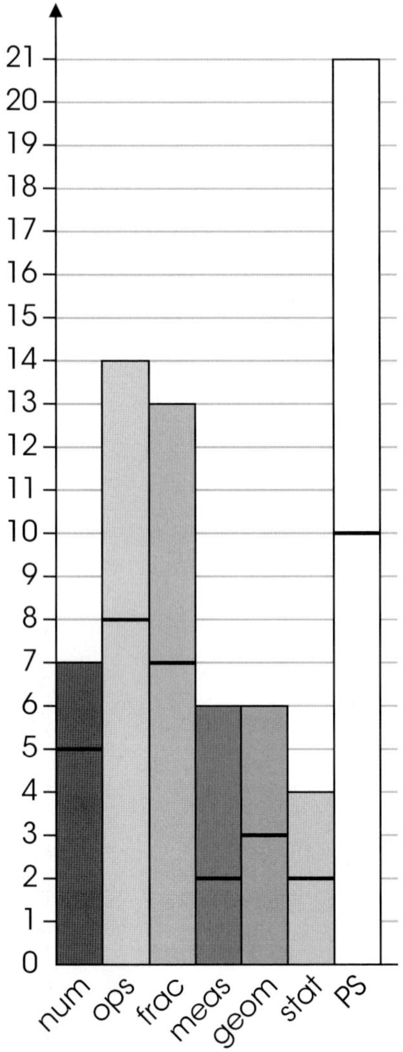

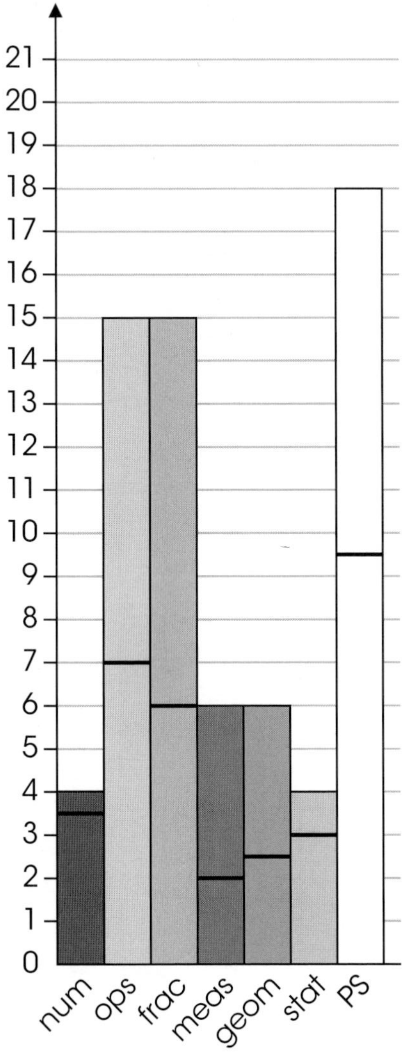

Photocopiable resource: this record sheet may be photocopied within the purchasing institution. Copyright © Hodder & Stoughton 2015.

4 Obtaining and interpreting test scores

Summative measures

Raw scores

A pupil's raw score is the total mark on a particular test. As an overview, you can compare how well a pupil has done by comparing his or her raw score to Table 4.1. This shows average raw scores for each *PUMA* test, by gender. You may also compare your class average raw scores against these averages.

Table 4.1: Average raw scores for each test by gender

	Combined Autumn test			Spring test			Summer test		
	Boys	Girls	Total	Boys	Girls	Total	Boys	Girls	Total
PUMA 3	18.6	17.9	18.3	19.3	19.1	19.3	21.6	20.0	20.7
PUMA 4	19.3	18.1	18.7	18.9	17.9	18.3	21.4	20.8	21.2
PUMA 5	21.4	19.8	20.6	23.0	20.1	21.7	20.9	18.2	19.7
PUMA 6	24.5	22.1	23.3	27.7	26.9	27.3	24.8	23.2	23.9

The results obtained from *PUMA* will also enable you to report pupil performance in terms of the following measures:

- standardised score (see tables in **Chapter 6**)
- age-standardised score (see tables in **Chapter 6**)
- percentile (Table **4.3**)
- mathematics age (Table **4.4**)
- Hodder Scale score (Tables **4.5** and **5.3**)
- end of year expectations thresholds (Appendix B).

Standardised scores, age-standardised scores and confidence bands

Both types of standardised score obtained from *PUMA* are standardised to an average score of 100, immediately showing whether a pupil is above or below average as compared to *PUMA's* national standardisation sample.

However, age-standardised scores take into account a pupil's age so that we can see how a pupil's test performance compares with other pupils *of the same age*, whereas standardised scores are for a year cohort and do not take age into account.

The advantage of using age-standardised scores for comparing summative performance, rather than standardised scores which do not reflect maturation, is that older pupils are likely to obtain *higher raw* scores than younger pupils but could still gain a *lower standardised* score. Therefore, using an age-standardised score enables you to rank pupils in order of achievement after age has been accounted for.

In Years 5 and 6, since teaching is likely to have a significant if not a greater impact on achievement than the chronological age and maturation of the child, standardised scores have a value too.

Standardised scores and age-standardised scores can both be averaged to give an indication of the general attainment level of a class or even a whole intake. This is especially helpful when exploring value-added, since schools with a very weak intake will be able to demonstrate where their pupils are making good progress.

By definition, age-standardised scores suggest that older children will do better than younger children. In most tests that span a number of years, this is indeed the case, as age and experience do matter. However, since the *PUMA* tests are written for each individual year group, our initial research found that age was not strongly correlated with performance. This is not surprising, as the pupils will all be receiving a fairly common experience based on the new curriculum, so progress is likely to be more reflective of innate ability and the quality of teaching, support and practice at school and at home. Therefore, to provide age differentiation in the standardisation, all pupils took two tests – that of their year group and that of the one-year-younger year group. Every test was therefore taken by a two-year age span cohort (apart from Year 1 in autumn and spring, and Reception which only took the one test in summer).

The standardised and age-standardised scores provided in Table 4.2 range between 70 and 130, with a mean of 100 and a standard deviation (SD) of 15. The SD tells you how spread out the scores are from the mean.

Using the SD and the 'normal distribution' of scores, pupils can be grouped by performance into bands. Figure 4.1 illustrates this grouping:

- Average refers to those whose performance is within one SD either side of the mean, i.e. 85–115).
- Below average and above average refer to those who are between one and two SDs either side of the mean, i.e. 70–85 and 115–130.

Figure 4.1: The normal distribution curve showing standard deviations, standardised and age-standardised scores, and percentiles

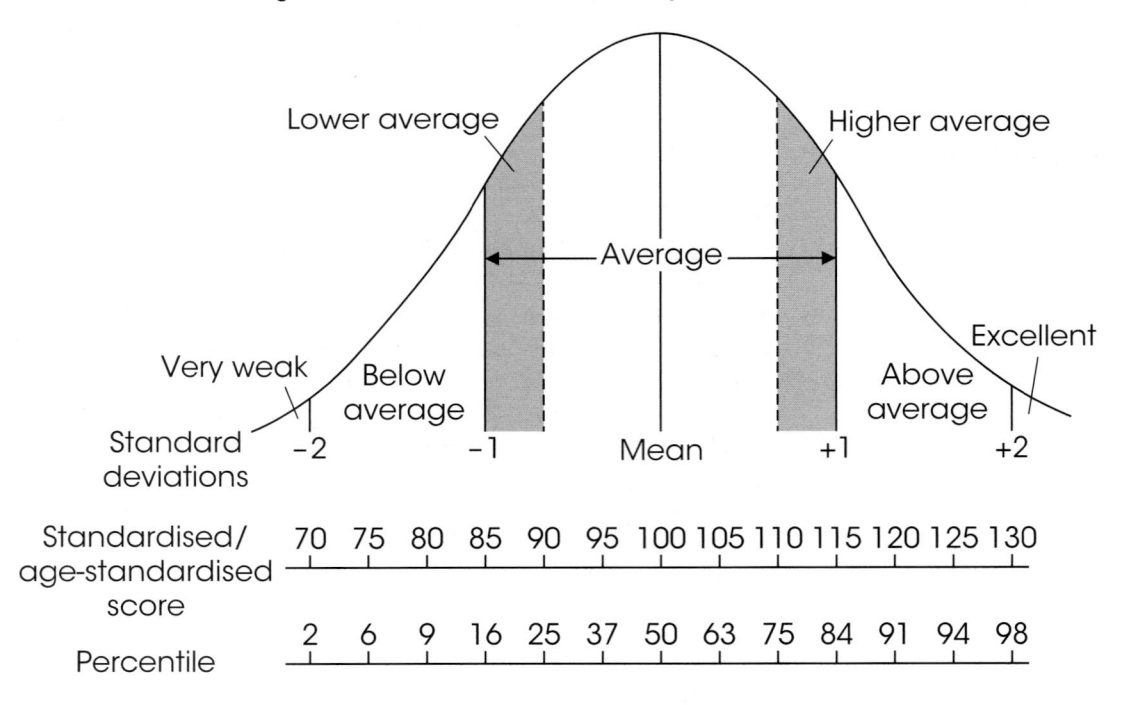

For many teachers, the term *average*, based on one SD either side of the mean is too wide a band, and so they prefer the *higher average* and *lower average* bands that are also shown on Figure 4.1 and in Table 4.2 below.

Table 4.2: Relationship between standardised/age-standardised test scores and qualitative interpretations

Standardised score	Qualitative interpretation of standardised scores	Standard deviation from mean	Percentile score	Percentage of normal population
>130	Excellent	>+2	>98	2.27
116–130	Above average	+1 to +2	84–98	13.59
110–115	*Higher average*			
85–115	Average/age-appropriate	−1 to +1	16–83	68.26
85–90	*Lower average*			
70–84	Below average	−1 to −2	2–15	13.59
<69	Very weak	<−2	<2	2.27

However, to suggest that one pupil is better than another and to place pupils in order of merit, you must be confident that the score obtained on the test is a 'true' score and therefore a true reflection of ability. A true score is always unknown because no test can be constructed to provide a perfect reflection of a person's ability. Therefore, tests often use confidence bands for each score to tell you how confident you can be that the score is a true score.

The *PUMA* tests use a 90% (or 95%) confidence band, which means that you can be 90% confident that the score is a pupil's true score. For example, for an age-standardised score of 106, if the confidence band is plus 6 and minus 6, you can be 90% confident that the pupil's 'true' score is between 100 and 112. The confidence bands are found in Table 5.2.

To obtain an age-standardised score, first calculate the pupil's chronological age in years and completed months and then refer to the conversion tables in Chapter 6. Record this on the front of the test booklet.

Percentiles

Percentiles can help to give you a feel for the significance of a pupil's score on a test, because they show the percentage in each age group who score below a certain level. So, an age-standardised score at the 68th percentile means that 68 per cent of the group scored below that particular pupil's age-standardised score. Thus the pupil falls in the top third for his or her age group.

Percentile scores may be derived from age-standardised scores. The relationship between age-standardised scores and percentiles is most easily seen by reference to Figure 4.1.

To obtain a pupil's percentile, first obtain his or her age-standardised score using the tables in Chapter 6, and then refer to Table 4.3 to obtain the percentile.

Table 4.3: Conversion of age-standardised scores to percentiles

Age-standardised score	Percentile	Age-standardised score	Percentile	Age-standardised score	Percentile
≥130	≥98	108	70	89	24
128–9	97	107	68	88	22
126–7	96	106	66	87	20
125	95	105	63	86	18
123–4	94	104	60	85	16
122	93	103	58	84	14
121	92	102	55	83	13
120	91	101	52	82	12
119	90	100	50	81	11
118	89	99	48	80	9
117	87	98	45	79	8
116	86	97	42	78	7
115	84	96	40	76–7	6
114	82	95	37	75	5
113	80	94	34	73–4	4
112	78	93	32	71–2	3
111	77	92	30	70	2
110	74	91	28	<70	1
109	72	90	26		

Thresholds for end of year performance indicators

There are two methods of using *PUMA* tests to provide information to assist teachers to ascribe a child's mark to a particular performance indicator. (Working towards, emerging, expected or exceeding are the terms we are using.)

One is derived from standardised scores obtained in the trials and relates to the cohort of children taking the tests in that term. The other method uses an algorithm and the facilities of the questions, applying a reasonable set of expectations, described below.

(Note: the facility indicates a child's success on a question. A high facility indicates an easy question and a low facility a difficult question. Facility may be given as a percentage or as a decimal. We use percentage.)

The tables of facilities for each test are given at the end of the manual in Appendix A. Appendix B contains tables with the thresholds for each test, which are derived using the algorithms and rationale explained below.

The first step in this empirically-based, theoretical process is to determine which category of difficulty it is appropriate to allocate to a question. We have used the following empirical information from the trials:

Category	Facility range
Working towards	90–100% success
Emerging	60–89% success
Expected	20–59% success
Exceeding	0–19% success

Our thinking behind the algorithm we use to establish the threshold for each category is:

> to be at the 'Expected' standard of performance children need to get 90% of the 'Emerging' questions of that term's test correct, over 60% of the 'Expected' questions correct, all of the 'Working towards' correct but none of the hard, 'Exceeding' questions.

There is no official definition or golden rule that gives us this. However, many years of working in test development (National Curriculum tests and optional tests, as well as commercial tests) and analysing related data have given us the considerable experience required to create algorithms that inform thresholds. The critical factor is that the rule we use has to have a sense of reasonableness; that is to say, it is based on our experience, together with discussions with a number of headteachers and numeracy/mathematics coordinators who concur with the thinking and methodology of creating a data-driven way to evolve thresholds.

Thresholds derived from these algorithms apply more to the curriculum age-expectation for the complete years than to a particular term. Therefore, in autumn they will be seen as very challenging and hard to achieve. Any child achieving the expected standard in autumn will be doing very well. The thresholds provide another way to monitor standards and progress. They should be used in conjunction with the thresholds derived from Standardised Scores, which relate to the term and will appear more generous (in effect, the standardised score information indicates whether children are on track to achieve that threshold in the summer not whether they are at the standard already).

The rules we have applied to derive each theoretical threshold are:

To be at the 'Expected' standard of performance:
Working towards   requires 100% of the marks at 90–100% facilities;
Emerging   90% of the marks at 60–89% facilities;
Expected   60% of the marks at 20–59% facilities;
Exceeding   0% of the marks at 0–19% facilities.

To be at the 'Emerging' standard of performance:
Working towards   requires 90% of the marks at 90–100% facilities;
Emerging   60% of the marks at 60–89% facilities;
Expected   0% of the marks at 20–59% facilities;
Exceeding   0% of the marks at 0–19% facilities.

To be at the 'Exceeding' standard of performance:
Working towards   requires 100% of the marks at 90–100% facilities;
Emerging   100% of the marks at 60–89% facilities;
Expected   90% of the marks at 20–59% facilities;
Exceeding   60% of the marks at 0–19% facilities.

Children who do not achieve above an emerging threshold are deemed to be at a 'Working towards' standard of performance regarding age-expectation for a year.

Teachers are thus able to utilise two methods of obtaining measures of standards of performance:

1. *the algorithmic method* described above, which produces challenging thresholds linked to performance in the summer, whatever term the test is taken in;

or

2. *the standardised score method*, which gives information about whether the child is on track to achieve the expected standard of performance at the end of the year. What is governing the SS thresholds here is a comparison of the child's mark and standardised score to the norms of the standardised score scale.

A simple way is to look up the marks and use the Standardised Scores in the table and assume that all children within the range 90–110 of the mean (i.e. 100) are at the appropriate age-expected stage in that term, and are on target to achieve the age-expected performance at the end of the year. Children below one standard deviation are likely to be classified as 'Working towards' and those between a SS of 85 and 90 could be classified as 'Emerging'. However, there must remain some hesitancy around the standardised score of 90; for example, a child obtaining a score close to 90 needs to have more than this one piece of information from a *PUMA* test for a teacher to make a professional judgement about their progress.

The advantage of having two different methods of helping to determine thresholds is that they provide independent sources of information for teachers to make their own professional judgement.

Mathematics ages

Many teachers use mathematics age as a quick reference. A mathematics age shows the *average* chronological age of the pupils who obtained each particular raw score, i.e. the chronological age at which this level of performance is typical. For more detailed comparative information, however, and especially for tracking progress over time, age-standardised scores and percentiles are preferable for the reasons outlined in the sections above.

Note that *PUMA* mathematics ages are provided for ages beyond the normal age range for a given year. These have been generated because almost all tests were taken by two consecutive year groups in the standardisation and we also undertook statistical extrapolations. Such extrapolations can be especially useful in interpreting the performance of less able pupils who have been given a test for a younger age range.

To obtain a pupil's mathematics age, use Table 4.4 and read across from the pupil's raw score to the appropriate column for the test taken. Record this on the front of the test booklet.

Table 4.4: Mathematics ages for each term

PUMA raw score	Mathematics age											PUMA raw score
	PUMA 3 Autumn	PUMA 3 Spring	PUMA 3 Summer	PUMA 4 Autumn	PUMA 4 Spring	PUMA 4 Summer	PUMA 5 Autumn	PUMA 5 Spring	PUMA 5 Summer	PUMA 6 Autumn	PUMA 6 Spring	PUMA 6 Summer	
1													1
2													2
3													3
4													4
5													5
6													6
7													7
8													8
9													9
10													10
11													11
12													12
13													13
14					<8:7		<9:3	<9:6				<10:1	14
15		<7:7			8:7		9:3	9:6	<9:10			10:1	15
16	<7:3	7:7	<7:8	<8:4	8:8		9:4	9:7	9:10			10:2	16
17	7:3	7:9	7:8	8:4	8:9		9:4	9:8	9:11			10:4	17
18	7:5	7:10	7:9	8:6	8:11	<8:10	9:5	9:9	10:1			10:5	18
19	7:7	8:0	7:11	8:8	9:0	8:10	9:7	9:10	10:2			10:7	19
20	7:9	8:2	8:1	8:10	9:2	8:10	9:8	9:11	10:4	<10:0		10:8	20
21	7:11	8:4	8:3	9:0	9:3	9:0	9:10	10:0	10:5	10:0		10:10	21
22	8:1	8:5	8:5	9:2	9:5	9:3	9:11	10:1	10:6	10:3	<10:1	11:0	22
23	8:3	8:7	8:7	9:4	9:6	9:5	10:0	10:3	10:8	10:7	10:1	11:1	23
24	8:5	8:9	8:9	9:6	9:8	9:8	10:2	10:4	10:9	10:10	10:3	11:3	24
25	8:7	8:10	8:10	9:8	9:9	9:10	10:3	10:5	10:10	11:2	10:5	11:5	25

PUMA raw score	Mathematics age											PUMA raw score
	PUMA 3 Autumn	PUMA 3 Spring	PUMA 3 Summer	PUMA 4 Autumn	PUMA 4 Spring	PUMA 4 Summer	PUMA 5 Autumn	PUMA 5 Spring	PUMA 5 Summer	PUMA 6 Autumn	PUMA 6 Spring	PUMA 6 Summer	
26	8:9	9:0	9:0	9:10	9:11	10:0	10:5	10:6	11:0	11:6	10:7	11:6	26
27	8:11	9:2	9:2	10:0	10:1	10:3	10:6	10:7	11:1	11:9	10:9	11:8	27
28	9:0	9:3	9:4	10:2	10:2	10:5	10:7	10:8	11:3	12:1	10:11	11:9	28
29	9:2	9:5	9:6	10:3	10:4	10:8	10:9	10:9	11:4	12:2	11:2	11:11	29
30	>9:2	9:7	9:8	>10:3	10:5	10:10	10:10	10:10	11:6	12:3	11:4	12:1	30
31		>9:7	9:10		10:7	>10:10	11:0	10:11	11:7	12:4	11:6	12:2	31
32			>9:10		>10:7		11:1	11:0	11:8	12:5	11:8	12:4	32
33							11:3	11:2	11:10	>12:5	11:11	12:6	33
34							>11:3	11:3	>11:10		12:1	12:7	34
35								11:4			12:3	>12:7	35
36								11:5			12:5		36
37								11:6			12:7		37
38								11:7			>12:7		38
39								>11:7					39
40													40
41													41
42													42
43													43
44													44
45													45
46													46
47													47
48													48
49													49
50													50

Hodder Scale scores

Refer to Tables 4.5 and 5.3 to obtain the Hodder Scale score for each pupil. This standardised scale is provided as a decimal scale from 0–6 and allows you to monitor the pupils' progress. It is also useful if the pupil falls outside the chronological age range of the age-standardised score table for the test used, because you may still obtain a score on the Hodder Scale.

Diagnostic and formative interpretation

Summative measures are valuable to provide an overall picture of the pupil's performance relative to his or her peers. Such data may confirm, for example, that the pupil is doing well for his or her age or against the cohort and may indicate that no intervention strategy is required. However, a more detailed check may show that good ability with numbers is masking a particular weakness in geometry or measures.

Use the profile to look for patterns of strengths and weaknesses

Every pupil has particular strengths and weaknesses across the curriculum that will show up in the *PUMA* profile. When you are marking, you can see at which point there is a change from mostly correct to mostly incorrect answers and at what level of demand this is occurring. This may alert you to generally weak achievement or perhaps to a weakness (or strength) in one specific aspect of mathematics. For example, such an exploration may highlight aspects of geometry, perhaps taught in earlier years, which have been forgotten or were not fully understood at the time. It should be borne in mind when undertaking this form of analysis that performance will naturally reflect recent teaching.

Check a pupil's performance on a specific question

It is also possible to compare how a particular pupil has performed relative to other pupils in the same year group. Appendix A shows what proportion of pupils in that year group answered each question correctly. This is called the **facility** and shows the percentage of the pupils in the national sample that answered each question correctly.

Obtaining patterns and predictions of performance

While *PUMA interactive* will make it easier to automatically pinpoint areas of strengths and weakness, the same analysis of patterns of performance is available for pupils taking the paper-and-pencil version of the tests. Total raw scores, the score for each question or the score for a category may be entered into the Assessment Plus online reporting tool; not only will the record then be held electronically, but a complete set of performance analyses will be carried out.

The programme also allows you to monitor progress in the strands of the Content Domains of the Test Framework and to track pupil progress term by term, plus *PUMA Digital Online* provides predictions of future performance and an opportunity to monitor against previous performance (see next section). Predictions of progress can also be obtained from Table 4.6.

The two case studies on pages 72 and 73 illustrate how this comparative information can inform the teacher's planning. With this more detailed picture, it is possible to implement specific teaching strategies to support the development of each pupil.

Reporting progress with the Hodder Scale

In developing the *PUMA* tests, seven cohorts of more than 1000 pupils each, totalling just under 8000 pupils, were tracked termly over four terms. Using this information and Optional and Key Stage test data along with Teacher Assessment, it was possible to link pupil performance from term to term and year to year. Identifying patterns in this way provides a firm basis on which to predict future performance and establish expectations.

Table 4.5 provides, for each test, a complete set of reference data for reporting progress in terms of Hodder Scale score. Read across from the pupil's raw score on a particular test to the Hodder Scale score in the outside columns. Record this score on the front of the test booklet. Table 4.5 also shows LA points scores. To assist teachers we have included even numbers as well as the odd numbers. The even numbers are the equivalent of being at the top of an old sublevel, so that smaller increments of progress may be monitored.

Table 4.5: Relating *PUMA* raw scores to different scales

Hodder Scale	PUMA raw score						LA points score	Hodder Scale
	PUMA 3 Autumn	PUMA 3 Spring	PUMA 3 Summer	PUMA 4 Autumn	PUMA 4 Spring	PUMA 4 Summer		
0.9			<5					0.9
1.0	<5	5	5	<3			8	1.0
1.1	5	5	6	3			8	1.1
1.2	5	5	6	3			8	1.2
1.3	6	6	7	4			9	1.3
1.4	6	6	7	4			9	1.4
1.5	6	6	8	4			10	1.5
1.6	6	6	8	4	<3	<6	10	1.6
1.7	7	7	9	5	3	6	11	1.7
1.8	7	7	9	5	3	6	11	1.8
1.9	8	8	9	5	3	6	12	1.9
2.0	9	9	10	6	4	7	13	2.0
2.1	10	9	10	7	5	7	13	2.1
2.2	11	10	10	8	6	7	14	2.2
2.3	12–13	11	11	9	7	8	15	2.3
2.4	14–15	12	12	9	7	8	15	2.4
2.5	16–17	13	12	10	8	9	16	2.5
2.6	18	14	13	11	8	9	16	2.6
2.7	18–20	15–16	14	12–13	9	10	17	2.7

Hodder Scale	PUMA raw score						LA points score	Hodder Scale
	PUMA 3 Autumn	PUMA 3 Spring	PUMA 3 Summer	PUMA 4 Autumn	PUMA 4 Spring	PUMA 4 Summer		
2.8	21	17–18	15–16	14	10	11–12	17	2.8
2.9	22	19–20	17	15	11	13	18	2.9
3.0	23–24	21	18	16–17	12–13	14	19	3.0
3.1	25	22–23	19–20	18–19	14	15	19	3.1
3.2	26	24	21–22	20–21	15	16	20	3.2
3.3	27	25	23	22	16	17	21	3.3
3.4	27	26	24	22	17–18	18	21	3.4
3.5	28	27	25-26	23	19–20	19–20	22	3.5
3.6	29	28	27	23	21	21	22	3.6
3.7	30–31	29–30	28–29	24–25	22	22	23	3.7
3.8	32	31–32	30–31	26	23	23	23	3.8
3.9	33	33–34	32–33	27	24	24	24	3.9
4.0	34	35	34	28	25	25	25	4.0
4.1	34	36	35	29	26	26	25	4.1
4.2	35	36	36	30	27	27	26	4.2
4.3	36	37	37	31	28–29	28	27	4.3
4.4	36	38	38	32	30	29	27	4.4
4.5	37	39	39	33	31	29	28	4.5
4.6	38–40	40	40	34	32	30	28	4.6
4.7				35	33	31–33	29	4.7
4.8				35	34	34–36	29	4.8
4.9				35	35	37	30	4.9
5.0				36–37	36–37	38	31	5.0
5.1				38–39	38–39	39	31	5.1
5.2				40	40	40	32	5.2
5.3							33	5.3
5.4							33	5.4
5.5							34	5.5
5.6							34	5.6
5.7							35	5.7
5.8							35	5.8
5.9							36	5.9
6.0							37	6.0

Note: Where a pupil's raw score links to more than one point on the Hodder Scale or LA points score, the highest point on the scale should be awarded. Although this sets a higher expectation for the pupil to achieve on the next test, this will ensure that the pupil has a challenging target to aim for.

Hodder Scale	PUMA raw score						LA points score	Hodder Scale
	PUMA 5 Autumn	PUMA 5 Spring	PUMA 5 Summer	PUMA 6 Autumn	PUMA 6 Spring	PUMA 6 Summer		
1.0							8	1.0
1.1							8	1.1
1.2							8	1.2
1.3							9	1.3
1.4							9	1.4
1.5							10	1.5
1.6	<3						10	1.6
1.7	3						11	1.7
1.8	3						11	1.8
1.9	3	<6	<3				12	1.9
2.0	4	6	3	1			13	2.0
2.1	4	6	3	2			13	2.1
2.2	5	6	3	3	<4		14	2.2
2.3	6	7	4	4	4		15	2.3
2.4	6	7	4	4	4		15	2.4
2.5	7	8	4	5	4		16	2.5
2.6	7	8	4	5	4	<4	16	2.6
2.7	8	9	5	6	5	4	17	2.7
2.8	9	9	5	7	6	4	17	2.8
2.9	10	10	5	8	7	4	18	2.9
3.0	11–12	11	6	9	8	5	19	3.0
3.1	13–14	12	7	10	9	6	19	3.1
3.2	15	12	8	11	10	7	20	3.2
3.3	16	13	9	12–13	11–12	8	21	3.3
3.4	17	14	10	14	13–14	9	21	3.4
3.5	18	15	10	15	15	9	22	3.5
3.6	19	16	11	16	16	10	22	3.6
3.7	20–21	17	12	17	17	11	23	3.7
3.8	22–23	18	13–14	18	18	12–13	23	3.8
3.9	24	19	15	19	19	14	24	3.9
4.0	25–26	20–21	16	20–21	20–21	15	25	4.0
4.1	27–28	22–23	17–18	22–23	22–23	16	25	4.1
4.2	29	24–25	19	24–25	24–25	17	26	4.2
4.3	30–31	26–27	20	26–27	26–27	18	27	4.3
4.4	32–33	28–29	21–22	28	28	19	27	4.4
4.5	34	30–31	23–24	29	29	20	28	4.5
4.6	35	32–33	25–26	30	30	21	28	4.6
4.7	36	34	27–29	31–32	31	22–23	29	4.7

Hodder Scale	PUMA raw score						LA points score	Hodder Scale
	PUMA 5 Autumn	PUMA 5 Spring	PUMA 5 Summer	PUMA 6 Autumn	PUMA 6 Spring	PUMA 6 Summer		
4.8	36	35	30–32	33	32	24–25	29	4.8
4.9	37	36	33–34	34	33	26	30	4.9
5.0	38–39	37	35–37	35–36	34	27–28	31	5.0
5.1	40	38	38–40	37–38	35–36	29–30	31	5.1
5.2	41	39	40–41	39	37–38	31	32	5.2
5.3	42	40	42–43	40	39	32	33	5.3
5.4	43	41	44–45	40	40	33–34	33	5.4
5.5	44	42–43	46	41	41	35–36	34	5.5
5.6	45	44–45	47	42	42	37	34	5.6
5.7	46–47	46–47	48	43–44	43	38–39	35	5.7
5.8	48–49	48–49	49	45–46	44	40–41	35	5.8
5.9	50	50	50	47–48	45	42–43	36	5.9
6.0				49–50	46–48	44–45	37	6.0
6.1					49–50	46–47	37	6.1
6.2						48–49	38	6.2
6.3						50	39	6.3

Note: Where a pupil's raw score links to more than one point on the Hodder Scale or LA points score, the highest point on the scale should be awarded. Although this sets a higher expectation for the pupil to achieve on the next test, this will ensure that the pupil has a challenging target to aim for.

Predicting future performance with the Hodder Scale

The questions in the tests for each term cover the range of demand appropriate to the year and term (see Appendix A and Table 1.1). As the tests have been designed to challenge the pupils around the level at which they are expected to be working, you may find that pupils obtain similar *raw scores* (and standardised/age-standardised scores) from term to term but that their *level of performance*, as shown by the Hodder Scale score, will continue to increase.

In Table 4.6 you can see at a glance the Hodder Scale score of a pupil in any one term, and then you can track to the next column to find the anticipated Hodder Scale score they will obtain if they make average progress.

Monitoring the difference between the actual Hodder Scale score and the predicted average Hodder Scale score enables you to see whether able children increasingly diverge from predicted progress or weaker children begin to converge toward average progress. The Hodder Scale develops throughout the school, so progress can be monitored from Reception and into Key Stage 1 and on into Key Stage 2.

Table 4.6: Monitoring and predicting progress from Year 2 Summer until Year 6 Summer on a term-by-term basis

					Average Hodder Scale score							
PUMA 2 Summer	PUMA 3 Autumn	PUMA 3 Spring	PUMA 3 Summer	PUMA 4 Autumn	PUMA 4 Spring	PUMA 4 Summer	PUMA 5 Autumn	PUMA 5 Spring	PUMA 5 Summer	PUMA 6 Autumn	PUMA 6 Spring	PUMA 6 Summer
											2.7	2.8
											2.9	3.1
											3.0	3.3
										2.5	3.1	3.5
										2.7	3.3	3.8
									2.5	2.8	3.4	3.9
									2.8	3.0	3.5	4.0
								2.3	2.9	3.2	3.7	4.1
								2.5	3.0	3.3	3.8	4.2
							2.0	2.7	3.1	3.4	3.9	4.3
							2.2	2.8	3.2	3.5	3.9	4.3
						2.0	2.3	2.9	3.3	3.6	4.0	4.4
						2.2	2.4	3.0	3.4	3.7	4.1	4.4
						2.3	2.5	3.1	3.5	3.8	4.2	4.5
						2.4	2.6	3.1	3.6	3.9	4.3	4.6
					1.8	2.5	2.6	3.1	3.6	4.0	4.3	4.6
					2.0	2.6	2.7	3.2	3.6	4.0	4.3	4.6
					2.1	2.7	2.8	3.3	3.7	4.1	4.4	4.7
				1.8	2.2	2.8	2.9	3.4	3.7	4.1	4.4	4.7
				1.9	2.3	2.8	2.9	3.4	3.7	4.1	4.4	4.7
			1.7	2.0	2.4	2.9	3.0	3.5	3.8	4.2	4.5	4.8
			1.8	2.1	2.5	3.0	3.1	3.5	3.8	4.2	4.5	4.8
		1.5	1.9	2.2	2.6	3.0	3.1	3.5	3.8	4.2	4.5	4.8
		1.6	2.0	2.3	2.7	3.1	3.2	3.6	3.9	4.3	4.6	4.8
		1.7	2.1	2.3	2.7	3.1	3.2	3.6	3.9	4.3	4.6	4.8
		1.8	2.2	2.4	2.7	3.2	3.3	3.7	3.9	4.3	4.6	4.8
	1.3	1.9	2.2	2.4	2.7	3.2	3.3	3.7	3.9	4.3	4.6	4.8
	1.4	1.9	2.3	2.5	2.8	3.2	3.3	3.7	3.9	4.3	4.6	4.8
1.2	1.5	2.0	2.4	2.6	2.9	3.3	3.4	3.8	4.0	4.4	4.7	4.9
1.3	1.6	2.1	2.4	2.6	2.9	3.3	3.4	3.8	4.0	4.4	4.7	4.9
1.4	1.7	2.2	2.5	2.7	3.0	3.3	3.4	3.8	4.0	4.4	4.7	4.9
1.5	1.8	2.3	2.6	2.8	3.1	3.4	3.5	3.8	4.0	4.4	4.7	4.9
1.6	1.9	2.3	2.6	2.8	3.1	3.4	3.5	3.8	4.0	4.4	4.7	4.9
1.7	2.0	2.4	2.7	2.9	3.2	3.5	3.6	3.9	4.1	4.5	4.8	4.9
1.8	2.1	2.5	2.8	3.0	3.2	3.5	3.6	3.9	4.1	4.5	4.8	4.9
1.9	2.2	2.6	2.8	3.0	3.2	3.5	3.6	3.9	4.1	4.5	4.8	4.9

4 Obtaining and interpreting test scores

Average Hodder Scale score												
PUMA 2 Summer	PUMA 3 Autumn	PUMA 3 Spring	PUMA 3 Summer	PUMA 4 Autumn	PUMA 4 Spring	PUMA 4 Summer	PUMA 5 Autumn	PUMA 5 Spring	PUMA 5 Summer	PUMA 6 Autumn	PUMA 6 Spring	PUMA 6 Summer
2.0–2.1	2.3	2.7	2.9	3.1	3.3	3.6	3.7	4.0	4.2	4.6	4.8	5.0
2.2	2.4	2.7	3.0	3.2	3.4	3.6	3.7	4.0	4.2	4.6	4.8	5.0
2.3	2.5	2.8	3.0	3.2	3.4	3.6	3.7	4.0	4.2	4.6	4.8	5.0
2.4	2.6	2.9	3.1	3.2	3.4	3.6	3.7	4.0	4.2	4.6	4.8	5.0
2.5	2.7	3.0	3.2	3.3	3.5	3.7	3.8	4.1	4.2	4.6	4.8	5.0
2.6	2.8	3.0	3.2	3.3	3.5	3.7	3.8	4.1	4.2	4.6	4.8	5.0
2.7	2.9	3.1	3.3	3.4	3.6	3.8	3.9	4.2	4.3	4.7	4.9	5.1
2.8	3.0	3.2	3.4	3.5	3.7	3.8	3.9	4.2	4.3	4.7	4.9	5.1
2.9	3.1	3.3	3.4	3.5	3.7	3.8	3.9	4.2	4.3	4.7	4.9	5.1
3.0–3.1	3.2	3.4	3.5	3.6	3.7	3.9	4.0	4.2	4.3	4.7	4.9	5.1
3.2	3.3	3.4	3.6	3.7	3.8	4.0	4.1	4.3	4.4	4.8	5.0	5.1
3.3	3.4	3.5	3.6	3.7	3.8	4.0	4.1	4.3	4.4	4.8	5.0	5.1
3.4	3.5	3.6	3.7	3.8	3.9	4.0	4.1	4.3	4.4	4.8	5.0	5.1
3.5	3.6	3.7	3.8	3.9	4.0	4.1	4.2	4.4	4.4	4.8	5.0	5.1
3.6	3.7	3.8	3.8	3.9	4.0	4.1	4.2	4.4	4.4	4.8	5.0	5.1
3.6	3.7	3.8	3.9	4.0	4.1	4.1	4.2	4.4	4.4	4.8	5.0	5.1
3.7	3.8	3.9	4.0	4.0	4.1	4.1	4.2	4.4	4.4	4.8	5.0	5.1
3.8	3.9	4.0	4.0	4.0	4.1	4.1	4.2	4.4	4.4	4.8	5.0	5.1
	4.0	4.1	4.1	4.1	4.2	4.2	4.3	4.5	4.5	4.9	5.1	5.2
		4.1	4.1	4.2	4.2	4.3	4.3	4.5	4.5	4.9	5.1	5.2
		4.2	4.2	4.2	4.2	4.3	4.3	4.5	4.5	4.9	5.1	5.2
			4.3	4.3	4.3	4.3	4.3	4.5	4.5	4.9	5.1	5.2
			4.4	4.4	4.4	4.4	4.4	4.6	4.6	4.9	5.1	5.2
				4.5	4.5	4.5	4.5	4.6	4.6	5.0	5.2	5.3
				4.5	4.6	4.6	4.6	4.7	4.7	5.1	5.2	5.3
				4.6	4.7	4.7	4.7	4.8	4.8	5.1	5.2	5.3
					4.7	4.7	4.7	4.9	4.9	5.2	5.3	5.4
					4.7	4.8	4.8	4.9	4.9	5.2	5.3	5.4
						4.8	4.8	5.0	5.0	5.3	5.4	5.5
							4.8	5.1	5.1	5.3	5.4	5.5
							4.9	5.2	5.2	5.4	5.5	5.5
							5.0	5.2	5.2	5.4	5.5	5.5
							5.1	5.2	5.2	5.5	5.6	5.6
							5.2	5.3	5.3–5.4	5.6	5.7	5.7
								5.4–5.5	5.5–5.6	5.7	5.8	5.8
								5.6	5.7–5.8	5.8	5.9	5.9
										5.9	6.0	6.0
											6.0	6.1
											6.1	6.2
												6.3

4 Obtaining and interpreting test scores

The information on Table 4.6 allows you to set targets for the future so that the 'value-added' over a term or year can be measured. This can be done for both individual pupils and whole classes.

Use Table 4.7 to predict performance from the beginning of an academic year to the end of the academic year to gain a snapshot of the likely performance over the year of a pupil or class. Look up the term in which the pupil took the test and look across the row to see the anticipated Hodder Scale score they should achieve if they follow the progress of an average pupil.

Table 4.7: Monitoring and predicting progress from autumn to summer within each year group

Average Hodder scale score			
PUMA 3 Autumn	*PUMA 3 Summer*	*PUMA 4 Autumn*	*PUMA 4 Summer*
1.0	1.9	1.0	2.0
1.1	2.0	1.1	2.1
1.2	2.0	1.2	2.2
1.3	2.1	1.3	2.3
1.4	2.2	1.4	2.3
1.5	2.3	1.5	2.4
1.6	2.3	1.6	2.5
1.7	2.4	1.7	2.6
1.8	2.5	1.8	2.6
1.9	2.6	1.9	2.7
2.0	2.6	2.0	2.8
2.1	2.7	2.1	2.9
2.2	2.8	2.2	2.9
2.3	2.9	2.3	3.0
2.4	3.0	2.4	3.1
2.5	3.0	2.5	3.1
2.6	3.1	2.6	3.2
2.7	3.2	2.7	3.3
2.8	3.3	2.8	3.4
2.9	3.3	2.9	3.4
3.0	3.4	3.0	3.5
3.1	3.5	3.1	3.6
3.2	3.6	3.2	3.6
3.3	3.6	3.3	3.7
3.4	3.7	3.4	3.8
3.5	3.8	3.5	3.9
3.6	3.9	3.6	3.9
3.7	3.9	3.7	4.0
3.8	4.0	3.8	4.1
3.9	4.1	3.9	4.1
4.0	4.2	4.0	4.2
4.1	4.2	4.1	4.3

Average Hodder scale score			
PUMA 3 Autumn	PUMA 3 Summer	PUMA 4 Autumn	PUMA 4 Summer
4.2	4.3	4.2	4.4
4.3	4.4	4.3	4.4
4.4		4.4	4.5
4.5		4.5	4.6
4.6		4.6	4.7
4.7		4.7	4.7
4.8		4.8	4.8
4.9		4.9	4.9
5.0		5.0	4.9
5.1		5.1	5.0
5.2		5.2	5.1

Average Hodder Scale Score			
PUMA 5 Autumn	PUMA 5 Summer	PUMA 6 Autumn	PUMA 6 Summer
1.0		1.0	
1.1		1.1	
1.2		1.2	
1.3		1.3	
1.4	2.6	1.4	
1.5	2.7	1.5	
1.6	2.7	1.6	
1.7	2.8	1.7	
1.8	2.9	1.8	
1.9	2.9	1.9	
2.0	3.0	2.0	3.0
2.1	3.1	2.1	3.1
2.2	3.2	2.2	3.2
2.3	3.2	2.3	3.3
2.4	3.3	2.4	3.3
2.5	3.4	2.5	3.4
2.6	3.4	2.6	3.5
2.7	3.5	2.7	3.6
2.8	3.6	2.8	3.7
2.9	3.6	2.9	3.7
3.0	3.7	3.0	3.8
3.1	3.8	3.1	3.9
3.2	3.8	3.2	4.0
3.3	3.9	3.3	4.0
3.4	4.0	3.4	4.1
3.5	4.1	3.5	4.2
3.6	4.1	3.6	4.3
3.7	4.2	3.7	4.4
3.8	4.3	3.8	4.4
3.9	4.3	3.9	4.5
4.0	4.4	4.0	4.6
4.1	4.5	4.1	4.7

Average Hodder Scale Score			
PUMA 5 Autumn	PUMA 5 Summer	PUMA 6 Autumn	PUMA 6 Summer
4.2	4.5	4.2	4.8
4.3	4.6	4.3	4.8
4.4	4.7	4.4	4.9
4.5	4.7	4.5	5.0
4.6	4.8	4.6	5.1
4.7	4.9	4.7	5.1
4.8	5.0	4.8	5.2
4.9	5.0	4.9	5.3
5.0	5.1	5.0	5.4
5.1	5.2	5.1	5.5
5.2	5.2	5.2	5.5
5.3	5.3	5.3	5.6
5.4	5.4	5.4	5.7
5.5	5.4	5.5	5.8
5.6	5.5	5.6	5.9
5.7		5.7	5.9
5.8		5.8	6.0
5.9		5.9	6.1
6.0		6.0	6.2

The case studies presented in the next section illustrate some of the benefits of mining the *PUMA* data.

Case studies

Case study 1

As the school's mathematics coordinator explains – in the light of the current expectations of the new mathematics curriculum, we have employed a maths specialist teacher from our local high school to teach small groups of pupils from Years 3, 4, 5 and 6. The expectation is that these pupils will benefit from extension activities to enrich their learning. We are using an analysis of the pupils' *PUMA* test responses to inform and adapt planning for all classes and to give specific information for our specialist teacher.

Overall, from the administration of the summer term test, responses have shown that more teaching is needed on fractions. Last week, this area was addressed from Year 1 upwards by all the teachers and pupils in a planned response to the challenge of the curriculum demand.

In summer Year 4, a pupil scored 35 out of 40, doing very well and obtaining an age-standardised score of 130 (she was only aged 9 years and 4 months). It was only when we looked at which questions she got wrong, that there was a clear indication that fractions were her *bête noir*. Here answers to questions 15, 18 and both parts of 29 were wrong. It seemed she could do the relationships between fractions and decimals, and understood decimals, but that somehow questions which involved manipulating numbers with reference to the 'horizontal line' seemed to be causing the problem. She was placed in the small group working with the high school teacher for specialist coaching to find what the problem was and then to find the solution.

Case study 2

We have a successful monitoring system which is led by the assessment coordinators at our school. A variety of assessment tools are used in the classes during the term to lead to a teacher-assessed termly level for each child in key subjects. Formal testing at the end of each term leads to a level for the term's work, age-standardised scores and points progress obtained from *PUMA* for every child, which are compared to the teacher's assessment.

Using this data and after discussions with the class teacher, groups or individual pupils are quickly identified and moved to appropriate working groups to challenge or support their learning. Individual children needing one-to-one intervention strategies are put on appropriate schemes to boost their confidence and levels of achievement. Analysis of test results sometimes identifies specific weaker areas which can be addressed.

(a) *PUMA* test results showed that one pupil (aged 8:7), with a raw score of 19, had a lower than average age-standardised score of 94 at the end of Year 3. This placed her at 3.1 on the Hodder Scale (19 LA points). Although her classwork was close to average, progress, as measured by the test, was lower than expected. There were no external/home circumstances to explain the results. The SENCO allocated a teaching assistant to boost the child's confidence, with a recognised intervention strategy (Catch Up) to address weaker areas in numeracy, as shown by the diagnostic bar chart.

The pupil was monitored over the first two terms of Year 4, and in the end of Spring test good progress had been achieved (a raw score of 22), with an age-standardised score of 101 (now aged 9:4) and a Hodder Scale of 3.7. This is an increase of 4 LA points to 23. We felt we could draw back with intervention, but she will be carefully monitored in class and by testing over the coming terms. We will use the Hodder Scale to help us predict what future performance should be.

Intervention was continued for another half term and the success was maintained. It will be carefully monitored in class by testing over the coming terms, aided by the Hodder Scale to help us predict what future performance should be.

The parents were involved in all decisions and were delighted to share his success as they saw his increased confidence in numeracy. The parents and teachers value the results from regular reliable testing and the school's quick reaction to results.

(b) Analysis of *PUMA* Autumn test results against question categories for another pupil revealed that the child's weakest area was Problem Solving. Plotting results on the bar chart gave a good visual indication of this problem area since fewer than half marks were obtained. Reading assessments for this child showed no problem with reading the questions, but extra one-to-one sessions with a teaching assistant to progress this area of numeracy improved her confidence. Regular analysis using *PUMA* continued over the following terms and indicated that the progress was being maintained.

5 Technical information

Standardisation sample

Overall, 37 schools took part in the standardisation of the *PUMA* tests. The participating schools are described in Table 5.1.

According to school performance data on the Department for Education (DfE) website, 81% of pupils nationally in 2012 achieved level 4 or above in English and mathematics in the Key Stage 2 national tests, while 79% did so in 2013.

The statistics on the DfE website for 2012 also show that 80.9% of pupils in the participating schools gained a level 4 or above in the Key Stage 2 national tests for 2012, with 28.5% of all these pupils gaining a level 5. Overall, therefore, the performance of the schools taking part in the *PUMA* standardisation is very closely representative of primary schools across the country.

Table 5.1: Description of schools in the standardisation, including home languages of pupils

Language mix of pupils	Demography of primary schools in standardisation trials			
	In large town/city	Suburban to town/city	Rural small town	Village
Only English as home language			3	3
Fewer than 5 different home languages	1	5	3	7
Between 6 and 19 different home languages	3	3	1	2
More than 20 home languages	4	2		
Totals	8	10	7	12

In total, 7258 pupils took part in the standardisation – that is, over 1000 per year group.

Reliability

The reliability of a test indicates whether or not similar results would be obtained from repeated administrations of the test with similar samples of pupils. An appropriate statistical measure of test reliability for *PUMA* is Cronbach's Alpha (α), which measures internal consistency reliability or how well the set of items measures mathematic skills in individuals in a consistent manner. A value above 0.60 is considered the minimum acceptable for most forms of educational assessment. This value for each test is presented in Table 5.2.

Table 5.2: Reliability measures

	Autumn 2013	Spring 2014	Summer 2014	Autumn 2014	Autumn combined
PUMA 3					
Y3 + Y4 sample size for age-standardised score	2050	2039	1974	1932	3982
Pearson correlation of Age with test score	0.40	0.38	0.36	0.30	0.3
Y3 number of children	1073	1090	1035	1133	
Y3 Boys	556	552	518	589	
Y3 Girls	517	538	517	544	
Y3 Mean mark /30	17.9	19.3	20.7	18.9	18.5
Y3 Cronbach Alpha	0.92	0.91	0.92	0.92	
Y3 90% confidence band for mean	±3.9	±4.1	±4.40	±3.93	
Y3 95% confidence band for mean	±4.86	±5.10	±5.04	±4.92	
Y3 Standard error of measurement	2.43	2.55	2.52	2.46	
PUMA 4					
Y4 + Y5 sample size for age-standardised score	1968	1949	1949	1667	3635
Pearson correlation of Age with test score	0.38	0.37	0.33	0.38	0.38
Y4 number of children	1055	1080	1070	1034	
Y4 Boys	510	534	530	508	
Y4 Girls	545	546	540	526	
Y4 Mean mark /40	18.3	18.3	21.2	19.13	18.7
Y4 Cronbach Alpha	0.90	0.92	0.90	0.91	
Y4 90% confidence band for mean	±3.9	±4.0	±3.9	±3.92	
Y4 95% confidence band for mean	±4.90	±5.02	±4.96	±4.90	
Y4 Standard error of measurement	2.45	2.51	2.48	2.45	
PUMA 5					
Y5 + Y6 sample size for age-standardised score	1960	1919	1751	1632	3592
Pearson correlation of age with test score	0.34	0.38	0.35	0.34	0.35
Y5 number of children	1047	1044	965	1038	
Y5 Boys	566	574	528	522	
Y5 Girls	481	470	437	516	
Y5 Mean mark /50	20.7	21.7	19.7	20.74	20.7
Y5 Cronbach Alpha	0.93	0.93	0.94	0.93	
Y5 90% confidence band for mean	±4.5	±4.6	±4.3	±4.59	
Y5 95% confidence band for mean	±5.68	±5.80	±5.48	±5.74	
Y5 Standard error of measurement	2.84	2.90	2.74	2.87	

	Autumn 2013	Spring 2014	Summer 2014	Autumn 2014	Autumn combined
PUMA 6					
Y6 sample size for age-standardised score	835	1020	894	892	1727
Pearson correlation of age with test score	0.08	−0.24	0.21	0.08	0.08
Y6 number of children	966	1039	917	943	
Y6 Boys	479	516	448	519	
Y6 Girls	487	523	469	424	
Y6 Mean mark /50	22.3	27.3	23.9	23.7	23.0
Y6 Cronbach Alpha	0.94	0.94	0.93	0.94	
Y6 90% confidence band for mean	±4.4	±4.4	±4.5	±4.32	
Y6 95% confidence band for mean	±5.5	±5.56	±5.64	±5.40	
Y6 Standard error of measurement	2.74	2.78	2.82	2.70	

The overall sample sizes are greater than the sum of the boys and girls as a few test booklets did not indicate gender and the pupils' names gave no clue.

Note: The autumn 2014 age-standardised and standardised scores were obtained from the combination of the autumn 2013 and autumn 2014 pupils

All test scores are subject to some margin of error. This does not imply that a child has been assessed incorrectly, but rather that we need to make a statistical estimate of the accuracy of the test as a measuring instrument. There are two ways of reporting this margin of error. One is the 90% confidence band and the other is the standard error of measurement (SEM). Using the confidence band, we can say that we are 90% confident that the child's 'true' score lies in a certain range around the obtained score (see also page 57). For example, for a child aged say 8:9 (eight years and nine months) who obtains a raw score of 24 marks on the *PUMA 3 Summer* test and hence an age-standardised score of 100, we can say with 90% confidence that their 'true' age-standardised score lies between 96 and 104. The confidence band for each test is presented in Table 5.2.

The SEM estimates how pupils' scores would be distributed around their true score if they took the test several times. The smaller the SEM the more reliable the score. The SEM for each test is also presented in Table 5.2.

Another measure used here is the Pearson coefficient. It is a measure of the closeness of a linear association between two variables, such as the relationship between age and raw score. Values over 0.3 indicate a more than acceptable closeness while above 0.5 indicates a strong closeness.

For tests targeting a particular age range, we use a standardisation method based on percentile norms – the fundamental principle being that scores at the same percentile rank are comparable. Hence a pupil at, say, the 30th percentile in his or her age group has the same relative ability as a pupil at the 30th percentile in any other age group. The standardisation procedure that we have used for these tests is called the *non-parallel linear regression model*.[1]

---

[1] Our basic methodology follows D.G. Lewis (see *Statistical Methods in Education*, University of London Press, 1972, pp. 86–96), with enhancements outlined by I. Schagen (see 'A Method for the Age Standardisation of Test Scores', *Applied Psychological Measurement*, 14, 4, December 1990, pp. 387–93) and Kiek, L.A. (*ESITEMS User Guide – Age Standardisation*, Cambridge University Local Examinations Syndicate, Research and Evaluation Division, 1997, p. 61.)

Correlation of teacher assessment to national tests

A sample of the participating schools provided both summer teacher assessment levels and former National Curriculum levels (from the national tests) for 200 Year 2 and 420 Year 6 children.

Correlation studies found that the teacher assessments were extremely close to the test levels the pupils obtained:

- At Key Stage 1 the correlation was 0.94, which is an extremely high correlation value (1.0 being a perfect match).

- At Key Stage 2 the correlation was 0.83, which is a very high correlation (normally correlation values of 0.3 are considered to represent reasonable correlation).

Since Key Stage 2 has six levels compared to the three levels used in Key Stage 1, Key Stage 2 allows for a bigger variation in both teachers' assessments and National Curriculum levels. Therefore, it is not surprising that the correlation of TA with National Curriculum levels at Key Stage 1 is slightly stronger than it is at Key Stage 2.

For both Key Stage 1 and Key Stage 2, the TA levels were a little more optimistic than their pupils' obtained National Curriculum test levels; at Key Stage 1, TA levels on average were about 0.1 of a level higher than National Curriculum levels, while at Key Stage 2 the TA levels were about 0.2 of a level higher. These differences are not statistically significant (as determined by paired samples t-tests on the means).

Validity

Strong face validity for a test like *PUMA* means that the test addresses the material in the curriculum which the pupils have studied and been taught. Each test in the *PUMA* series from Reception to Year 6 has been written to follow the Curriculum Maps. This ensures that these tests, which should ideally be taken toward the end of each term, meet the validity criterion. Table 5.3 shows how the *PUMA* tests map onto the Hodder Scale of demand.

The validity of the age standardisation is improved if there is a good correlation between the pupils' test scores and age, as demonstrated here by the Pearson correlations in Table 5.2. Additionally, the test itself must have high reliability (see above), so that the results would be replicated by repeated administrations of the test.

Table 5.3: *PUMA* tests analysed for range of mathematics demand

	P scales			Hodder Scale of demand																	
	P6	P7	P8	Low 1	Mid 1	High 1	Low 2	Mid 2	High 2	Low 3	Mid 3	High 3	Low 4	Mid 4	High 4	Low 5	Mid 5	High 5	6	Total
PUMA R Summer	2	1	4	7	8	7	1													30
PUMA 1 Autumn	1	1	1	10	4	3	6	3	1											30
PUMA 1 Spring				2	10	9	4	2	3											30
PUMA 1 Summer				6	8	5	3	3	4	1										30
PUMA 2 Autumn			1	3	6	3	5	3	7	1	1									30
PUMA 2 Spring				2	3	2	6	1	6	4	4	2								30
PUMA 2 Summer						2	5	8	4	8	2	1								30
PUMA 3 Autumn					1	2	8	6	3	3	6	9	1	1						40
PUMA 3 Spring							5	4	7	5	9	6	2	2						40
PUMA 3 Summer							3	4	4	11	9	5	2	2						40
PUMA 4 Autumn							4	4	6	7	4	5	6	4						40
PUMA 4 Spring								3	3	7	10	7	5	5	1					40
PUMA 4 Summer									2	13	6	5	3	9	2					40
PUMA 5 Autumn									5	6	9	7	3	8	7	5				50
PUMA 5 Spring										1	10	8	8	6	9	4	2	2		50
PUMA 5 Summer										5	5	3	9	6	7	5	5	5		50
PUMA 6 Autumn										6	9	6	7	5	5	2	4	3	3	50
PUMA 6 Spring										1	4	4	12	9	2	4	3	5	6	50
PUMA 6 Summer										2	3	2	5	6	12	6	6	1	7	50

PUMA 6 Autumn: Standardised scores

Raw score	Standardised score
1	71
2	72
3	73
4	74
5	76
6	77
7	78
8	80
9	81
10	82
11	84
12	85
13	86
14	88
15	89
16	90
17	92
18	93
19	94
20	96
21	97
22	98
23	100
24	101
25	102
26	104
27	105
28	106
29	108
30	109
31	110
32	112
33	113
34	114
35	116
36	117
37	118
38	120
39	121
40	122
41	124
42	125
43	126
44	127
45	129
46	130
47	131
48	133
49	134
50	135

PUMA 6 Spring: Standardised scores

Raw score	Standardised score
1	64
2	66
3	67
4	68
5	70
6	71
7	73
8	74
9	75
10	77
11	78
12	79
13	81
14	82
15	84
16	85
17	86
18	88
19	89
20	90
21	92
22	93
23	95
24	96
25	97
26	99
27	100
28	101
29	103
30	104
31	106
32	107
33	108
34	110
35	111
36	112
37	114
38	115
39	117
40	118
41	119
42	121
43	122
44	123
45	125
46	126
47	128
48	129
49	130
50	132

PUMA 6 Summer: Standardised scores

Raw score	Standardised score
1	66
2	68
3	70
4	71
5	73
6	74
7	76
8	77
9	78
10	80
11	81
12	83
13	84
14	86
15	87
16	88
17	90
18	91
19	93
20	94
21	96
22	97
23	99
24	100
25	101
26	103
27	104
28	106
29	107
30	109
31	110
32	111
33	113
34	114
35	116
36	117
37	119
38	120
39	122
40	123
41	124
42	126
43	127
44	129
45	130
46	132
47	133
48	134
49	136
50	137

PUMA 5 Autumn: Standardised scores

Raw score	Standardised score
1	73
2	75
3	76
4	77
5	79
6	80
7	81
8	83
9	84
10	85
11	87
12	88
13	90
14	91
15	92
16	94
17	95
18	96
19	98
20	99
21	101
22	102
23	103
24	105
25	106
26	107
27	109
28	110
29	112
30	113
31	114
32	116
33	117
34	118
35	120
36	121
37	122
38	124
39	125
40	127
41	128
42	129
43	131
44	132
45	133
46	135
47	136
48	138
49	139
50	140

PUMA 5 Spring: Standardised scores

Raw score	Standardised score
1	72
2	73
3	75
4	76
5	77
6	79
7	80
8	81
9	83
10	84
11	86
12	87
13	88
14	90
15	91
16	92
17	94
18	95
19	96
20	98
21	99
22	100
23	102
24	103
25	104
26	106
27	107
28	108
29	110
30	111
31	113
32	114
33	115
34	117
35	118
36	119
37	121
38	122
39	123
40	125
41	126
42	127
43	129
44	130
45	131
46	133
47	134
48	135
49	136
50	137

PUMA 5 Summer: Standardised scores

Raw score	Standardised score
1	74
2	76
3	77
4	78
5	80
6	81
7	83
8	84
9	85
10	87
11	88
12	89
13	91
14	92
15	94
16	95
17	96
18	98
19	99
20	100
21	102
22	103
23	105
24	106
25	107
26	109
27	110
28	111
29	113
30	114
31	116
32	117
33	118
34	120
35	121
36	122
37	124
38	125
39	127
40	128
41	129
42	131
43	132
44	133
45	135
46	136
47	138
48	139
49	140
50	142

PUMA 4 Autumn: Standardised scores

Raw score	Standardised score
1	67
2	69
3	71
4	73
5	75
6	77
7	78
8	80
9	82
10	84
11	86
12	88
13	90
14	91
15	93
16	95
17	97
18	99
19	101
20	103
21	104
22	106
23	108
24	110
25	112
26	114
27	116
28	117
29	119
30	121
31	123
32	125
33	127
34	129
35	130
36	132
37	134
38	136
39	138
40	140

PUMA 4 Spring: Standardised scores

Raw score	Standardised score
1	71
2	73
3	74
4	76
5	78
6	79
7	81
8	83
9	84
10	86
11	88
12	89
13	91
14	92
15	94
16	96
17	97
18	99
19	101
20	102
21	104
22	106
23	107
24	109
25	111
26	112
27	114
28	115
29	117
30	119
31	120
32	122
33	124
34	125
35	127
36	129
37	130
38	132
39	133
40	135

PUMA 4 Summer: Standardised scores

Raw score	Standardised score
1	62
2	64
3	66
4	68
5	70
6	71
7	73
8	75
9	77
10	79
11	81
12	83
13	85
14	86
15	88
16	90
17	92
18	94
19	96
20	98
21	100
22	102
23	103
24	105
25	107
26	109
27	111
28	113
29	115
30	117
31	119
32	120
33	122
34	124
35	126
36	128
37	130
38	132
39	134
40	136

6 Standardised score tables

Standardised scores for *PUMA*

PUMA 3 Autumn: Standardised scores

Raw score	Standardised score
1	70
2	72
3	74
4	75
5	77
6	79
7	80
8	82
9	84
10	86
11	87
12	89
13	91
14	93
15	94
16	96
17	98
18	100
19	101
20	103
21	105
22	107
23	108
24	110
25	112
26	114
27	115
28	117
29	119
30	120
31	122
32	124
33	126
34	127
35	129
36	131
37	133
38	134
39	136
40	138

PUMA 3 Spring: Standardised scores

Raw score	Standardised score
1	67
2	69
3	71
4	73
5	74
6	76
7	78
8	80
9	82
10	83
11	85
12	87
13	89
14	91
15	92
16	94
17	96
18	98
19	99
20	101
21	103
22	105
23	107
24	108
25	110
26	112
27	114
28	116
29	117
30	119
31	121
32	123
33	125
34	126
35	128
36	130
37	132
38	133
39	135
40	137

PUMA 3 Summer: Standardised scores

Raw score	Standardised score
1	66
2	68
3	69
4	71
5	73
6	75
7	76
8	78
9	80
10	81
11	83
12	85
13	87
14	88
15	90
16	92
17	93
18	95
19	97
20	99
21	100
22	102
23	104
24	106
25	107
26	109
27	111
28	112
29	114
30	116
31	118
32	119
33	121
34	123
35	124
36	126
37	128
38	130
39	131
40	133

Age-standardised scores for PUMA

PUMA 3 Autumn: Age-standardised scores

Raw score	7:3	7:4	7:5	7:6	7:7	7:8	7:9	7:10	7:11	8:0	8:1	8:2	8:3	8:4	8:5	8:6	8:7	8:8	8:9	8:10	8:11	9:0	9:1	9:2	Raw score
1																									1
2	70																								2
3	74	72	71	70																					3
4	77	76	75	73	72	71	70																		4
5	79	78	77	76	75	74	73	72	71	70															5
6	81	81	80	79	78	77	76	75	74	73	72	71	70												6
7	83	82	82	81	80	79	78	77	76	76	75	74	72	71											7
8	85	84	83	83	82	81	80	79	78	78	77	76	75	74	73	72	71	70							8
9	87	86	85	84	83	83	82	81	80	80	79	78	77	76	76	75	74	73	72	71	70	70			9
10	89	88	87	86	85	84	83	83	82	81	81	80	79	78	77	77	76	75	75	74	73	72	71	70	10
11	90	90	89	88	87	86	85	84	84	83	82	81	81	80	79	78	78	77	76	76	75	74	73	73	11
12	92	91	90	90	89	88	87	86	85	84	84	83	82	82	81	80	79	79	78	77	77	76	76	75	12
13	93	93	92	91	90	90	89	88	87	86	85	84	84	83	82	82	81	80	80	79	78	78	77	76	13
14	95	94	93	93	92	91	90	89	89	88	87	86	85	84	84	83	82	82	81	81	80	79	79	78	14
15	97	96	95	94	93	92	92	91	90	89	89	88	87	86	85	84	84	83	83	82	81	81	80	79	15
16	98	97	97	96	95	94	93	92	92	91	90	89	89	88	87	86	85	85	84	83	83	82	81	81	16
17	100	99	98	97	96	96	95	94	93	92	92	91	90	89	89	88	87	86	85	85	84	83	83	82	17
18	101	100	100	99	98	97	96	96	95	94	93	92	92	91	90	89	89	88	87	86	85	85	84	83	18
19	103	102	101	100	100	99	98	97	96	96	95	94	93	92	91	91	90	89	89	88	87	86	85	85	19
20	104	103	103	102	101	100	99	99	98	97	96	96	95	94	93	92	91	91	90	89	89	88	87	86	20
21	105	105	104	103	103	102	101	100	99	99	98	97	96	96	95	94	93	92	91	91	90	89	89	88	21
22	107	106	106	105	104	103	103	102	101	100	99	99	98	97	96	96	95	94	93	92	91	91	90	89	22
23	109	108	107	107	106	105	104	103	103	102	101	100	99	99	98	97	96	95	95	94	93	92	91	91	23
24	110	109	109	108	108	107	106	105	104	103	103	102	101	100	99	99	98	97	96	95	95	94	93	92	24
25	111	111	110	110	109	108	108	107	106	105	104	104	103	102	101	100	99	99	98	97	96	95	95	94	25

Award < 69 for all scores in this area

Raw score	Age in years and completed months																							Raw score
	7:3	7:4	7:5	7:6	7:7	7:8	7:9	7:10	7:11	8:0	8:1	8:2	8:3	8:4	8:5	8:6	8:7	8:8	8:9	8:10	8:11	9:0	9:1	9:2	
26	113	112	112	111	111	110	109	109	108	107	106	105	104	104	103	102	101	100	99	99	98	97	96	95	26
27	114	114	113	113	112	111	111	110	110	109	108	107	106	106	105	104	103	102	101	100	99	99	98	97	27
28	116	115	115	114	114	113	112	112	111	111	110	109	108	108	107	106	105	104	103	102	101	100	99	99	28
29	117	117	116	116	115	115	114	113	113	112	112	111	110	109	109	108	107	106	105	104	103	102	102	100	29
30	119	119	118	118	117	116	116	115	115	114	113	113	112	111	110	110	109	108	107	106	105	104	103	102	30
31	121	120	120	119	119	118	118	117	116	116	115	114	114	113	112	112	111	110	109	108	107	106	105	104	31
32	123	122	122	121	121	120	120	119	118	118	117	116	116	115	114	114	113	112	111	110	110	109	108	107	32
33	125	124	124	123	123	122	122	121	121	120	119	119	118	117	117	116	115	114	113	113	112	111	110	109	33
34	127	126	126	126	125	125	124	124	123	122	122	121	120	120	119	118	117	117	116	115	114	113	112	111	34
35	129	128	128	128	127	127	126	126	125	125	124	124	123	122	122	121	120	119	118	118	117	116	115	114	35
36		131	130	130	130	129	129	128	128	128	127	127	126	125	125	124	123	123	122	121	120	119	118	117	36
37									131	130	130	129	129	128	128	127	127	126	125	124	123	123	122	120	37
38																131	130	130	129	128	128	127	126	125	38
39					Award > 131 for all scores in this area																		130	129	39
40																									40
	7:3	7:4	7:5	7:6	7:7	7:8	7:9	7:10	7:11	8:0	8:1	8:2	8:3	8:4	8:5	8:6	8:7	8:8	8:9	8:10	8:11	9:0	9:1	9:2	

6 Standardised score tables

PUMA 3 Spring: Age-standardised scores

Raw score	7:7	7:8	7:9	7:10	7:11	8:0	8:1	8:2	8:3	8:4	8:5	8:6	8:7	8:8	8:9	8:10	8:11	9:0	9:1	9:2	9:3	9:4	9:5	9:6	9:7	Raw score
1	70																									1
2	73	71	70																							2
3	76	74	73	71																						3
4	78	77	75	74	72	70																				4
5	81	79	78	76	75	73	72	70																		5
6	83	82	80	79	77	76	74	73	71	70																6
7	85	84	82	81	80	78	77	75	74	72	71															7
8	87	86	84	83	82	81	79	78	76	75	73	72	70													8
9	89	87	86	85	84	83	81	80	79	77	76	74	73	71	70											9
10	90	89	88	87	86	85	83	82	81	80	78	77	75	74	72	71	69									10
11	92	91	90	89	88	86	85	84	83	82	80	79	78	76	75	73	72	71								11
12	94	93	91	90	89	88	87	86	85	84	82	81	80	79	77	76	74	73	72	70						12
13	95	94	93	92	91	90	89	88	87	85	84	83	82	81	79	78	77	75	74	73	71	70				13
14	97	96	95	94	93	92	91	90	88	87	86	85	84	83	82	80	79	78	76	75	74	72	71			14
15	99	98	97	96	95	94	92	91	90	89	88	87	86	85	83	82	81	80	78	77	76	75	73	69	70	15
16	100	99	99	98	96	95	94	93	92	91	90	89	88	86	85	84	83	82	81	79	78	77	75	72	73	16
17	102	101	100	99	98	97	96	95	94	93	92	90	89	88	87	86	85	84	82	81	80	79	78	74	75	17
18	103	103	102	101	100	99	98	97	96	95	93	92	91	90	89	88	87	85	84	83	82	81	80	76	77	18
19	105	104	103	102	101	100	100	99	97	96	95	94	93	92	91	90	88	87	86	85	84	83	82	78	79	19
20	107	106	105	104	103	102	101	100	99	98	97	96	95	94	92	91	90	89	88	87	86	85	83	80	81	20
21	108	107	106	106	105	104	103	102	101	100	99	98	97	95	94	93	92	91	90	89	87	86	85	82	83	21
22	109	109	108	107	106	105	104	103	103	102	101	100	99	97	96	95	94	93	92	90	89	88	87	84	85	22
23	111	110	109	109	108	107	106	105	104	103	102	101	100	99	98	97	96	95	93	92	91	90	89	86	87	23

Award <69 for all scores in this area

Age in years and completed months

Raw score	7:7	7:8	7:9	7:10	7:11	8:0	8:1	8:2	8:3	8:4	8:5	8:6	8:7	8:8	8:9	8:10	8:11	9:0	9:1	9:2	9:3	9:4	9:5	9:6	9:7	Raw score
24	112	112	111	110	109	108	108	107	106	105	104	103	102	101	100	99	98	96	95	94	93	92	91	90	88	24
25	114	113	112	112	111	110	109	108	108	107	106	105	104	103	102	101	100	99	97	96	95	94	92	91	90	25
26	115	115	114	113	112	112	111	110	109	108	108	107	106	105	103	102	101	100	99	98	97	96	95	93	92	26
27	118	117	116	115	114	113	113	112	111	110	109	108	107	105	106	104	103	102	101	100	99	98	96	95	94	27
28	120	119	118	117	116	115	114	114	113	112	111	110	109	108	107	106	105	104	103	102	101	100	99	97	96	28
29	121	121	120	119	118	117	116	115	114	114	113	112	111	110	109	108	107	106	105	104	103	102	100	99	98	29
30	123	123	122	121	120	120	119	118	117	116	115	114	113	112	111	110	109	108	107	106	105	103	102	101	100	30
31	125	125	124	123	122	122	121	120	119	118	117	116	115	114	113	112	111	110	109	108	107	106	105	103	102	31
32	128	127	126	125	125	124	123	122	121	121	120	119	117	116	115	114	113	112	111	110	109	108	107	106	104	32
33	130	129	129	128	127	126	125	124	124	123	122	121	120	119	118	117	115	114	113	112	111	110	109	108	107	33
34				130	130	129	128	127	126	125	124	124	123	122	121	120	118	117	116	115	113	112	111	110	109	34
35								130	129	128	127	126	125	124	123	122	121	120	119	118	116	115	114	112	111	35
36											130	130	129	128	126	125	124	123	122	121	120	118	117	115	114	36
37			Award >130 for all scores in this are												130	129	128	127	125	124	123	122	120	119	117	37
38																		130	129	128	127	125	124	123	121	38
39																						130	128	127	125	39
40																									130	40
	7:7	7:8	7:9	7:10	7:11	8:0	8:1	8:2	8:3	8:4	8:5	8:6	8:7	8:8	8:9	8:10	8:11	9:0	9:1	9:2	9:3	9:4	9:5	9:6	9:7	

PUMA 3 Summer: Age-standardised scores

Raw score	7:8	7:9	7:10	7:11	8:0	8:1	8:2	8:3	8:4	8:5	8:6	8:7	8:8	8:9	8:10	8:11	9:0	9:1	9:2	9:3	9:4	9:5	9:6	9:7	9:8	9:9	9:10	Raw score
1																												1
2		70																										2
3	71		72	71	70																							3
4	75	73	75	74	73	72	71	70																				4
5	78	76	78	77	76	75	74	73	72	71	70																	5
6	81	79	81	80	78	77	76	75	74	73	72	71																6
7	84	82	84	82	81	80	79	78	77	76	75	74	73	72	71		70											7
8	86	85	86	85	84	82	81	80	79	78	77	76	75	74	73	71	72		71	70				69				8
9	88	87	88	87	86	85	84	82	81	80	79	78	77	76	75	73	74	69	72	70	69							9
10	89	88	89	88	88	87	86	85	84	82	81	80	79	78	77	75	76	71	71	72	71	71	70	71	71	70	70	10
11	91	90	91	90	89	88	87	87	86	85	84	83	81	80	80	77	78	73	72	74	73	72	72	73	72	72	70	11
12	92	92	92	91	91	90	89	88	87	86	86	85	84	83	82	79	80	75	74	75	75	74	73	74	74	73	71	12
13	94	93	94	93	92	91	90	89	89	88	87	86	86	85	84	81	82	77	76	77	76	76	75	76	75	74	73	13
14	95	94	95	94	93	93	92	91	90	89	89	88	87	86	85	83	84	79	78	79	78	77	77	78	77	75	74	14
15	97	96	97	96	95	94	93	93	92	91	90	90	89	88	86	85	86	81	80	81	80	79	78	79	79	76	76	15
16	98	98	98	98	97	96	95	94	93	92	92	91	90	89	87	86	87	83	82	83	82	81	80	81	80	78	77	16
17	100	99	100	99	98	97	97	96	95	94	93	92	92	91	89	88	88	85	84	85	84	83	82	83	82	79	79	17
18	101	101	101	100	100	99	98	97	96	95	95	94	93	92	90	89	90	86	85	86	85	85	84	85	84	81	80	18
19	103	102	103	102	101	100	100	99	98	97	96	95	94	94	91	91	91	88	87	88	87	86	85	86	85	83	82	19
20	104	103	104	103	103	102	101	100	99	99	98	97	96	95	93	92	93	91	88	89	88	88	87	87	87	85	84	20
21	106	105	106	104	104	103	103	102	101	100	99	99	98	97	94	93	94	92	91	90	90	89	88	88	88	86	85	21
22	107	106	106	105	104	103	103	102	101	100	99	99	98	97	96	95	94	93	92	92	91	90	90	89	88	87	87	22

Award <69 for all scores in this area

Age in years and completed months

Raw score	7:8	7:9	7:10	7:11	8:0	8:1	8:2	8:3	8:4	8:5	8:6	8:7	8:8	8:9	8:10	8:11	9:0	9:1	9:2	9:3	9:4	9:5	9:6	9:7	9:8	9:9	9:10	Raw score
23	108	108	107	107	106	105	104	103	103	102	101	100	99	99	98	97	96	95	94	93	92	92	91	90	89	89	88	23
24	110	109	109	108	107	107	106	105	104	103	103	102	101	100	99	98	98	97	96	95	94	93	92	91	91	90	89	24
25	111	111	110	109	109	108	107	107	106	105	104	103	103	102	101	100	99	98	97	96	95	94	94	93	92	91	91	25
26	112	112	111	111	110	110	109	108	108	107	106	105	104	103	103	102	101	100	99	98	97	96	95	94	93	93	92	26
27	114	113	113	112	112	111	110	110	109	108	108	107	106	105	104	103	102	102	101	100	99	98	97	96	95	94	93	27
28	115	115	114	114	113	112	112	111	111	110	109	109	108	107	106	105	104	103	102	102	101	100	99	98	97	96	95	28
29	117	116	116	115	115	114	113	113	112	112	111	110	110	109	108	107	106	105	104	103	102	101	100	100	99	98	97	29
30	118	118	117	117	116	116	115	114	114	113	113	112	111	111	110	109	108	107	106	105	104	103	102	101	100	99	99	30
31	120	120	119	118	118	117	117	116	115	115	114	114	113	112	112	111	110	109	108	108	107	105	104	103	102	101	100	31
32	123	122	121	121	120	119	119	118	118	117	116	115	115	114	113	113	112	111	110	110	109	108	107	106	104	103	102	32
33	125	125	124	123	123	122	121	121	120	119	118	118	117	116	115	115	114	113	112	112	111	110	109	108	107	106	104	33
34	128	128	127	126	126	125	124	124	123	122	121	120	119	119	118	117	116	115	115	114	113	112	111	110	109	108	107	34
35		131	130	130	129	128	128	127	126	125	125	124	123	122	121	120	119	118	117	116	115	115	114	113	112	111	109	35
36								131	130	129	129	128	127	126	125	124	123	122	121	120	119	118	117	115	114	113	112	36
37														131	130	129	128	127	126	125	123	122	121	119	118	117	115	37
38	Award >131 for all scores in this area																			131	130	128	127	125	124	122	120	38
39																										131	129	39
40																												40
Raw score	7:8	7:9	7:10	7:11	8:0	8:1	8:2	8:3	8:4	8:5	8:6	8:7	8:8	8:9	8:10	8:11	9:0	9:1	9:2	9:3	9:4	9:5	9:6	9:7	9:8	9:9	9:10	Raw score

6 Standardised score tables

PUMA 4 Autumn: Age-standardised scores

Raw score	8:3	8:4	8:5	8:6	8:7	8:8	8:9	8:10	8:11	9:0	9:1	9:2	9:3	9:4	9:5	9:6	9:7	9:8	9:9	9:10	9:11	10:0	10:1	10:2	Raw score
1																									1
2																									2
3	71	70																							3
4	74	73	71	70																					4
5	77	76	75	73	72	71	69																		5
6	80	79	77	76	75	74	72	71	70																6
7	82	81	80	79	77	76	75	74	73	71															7
8	85	83	82	81	80	79	78	76	75	74	73	72	71	70											8
9	87	86	85	83	82	81	80	79	78	77	76	74	73	72	71	70									9
10	89	88	87	86	85	83	82	81	80	79	78	77	76	75	74	72	71	70							10
11	90	89	89	88	87	86	85	83	82	81	80	79	78	77	76	75	74	73	72	71	70				11
12	92	91	90	89	88	88	87	86	85	83	82	81	80	79	78	77	76	75	74	73	72	70	69		12
13	94	93	92	91	90	89	88	88	87	86	85	83	82	81	80	79	78	77	76	75	74	72	71	71	13
14	96	95	94	93	92	91	90	89	88	87	86	86	85	83	82	81	80	79	78	77	76	75	74	73	14
15	97	97	96	95	94	93	92	91	90	89	88	87	86	85	85	84	82	82	81	80	79	77	76	75	15
16	99	98	97	96	96	95	94	93	92	91	90	89	88	87	86	85	85	84	83	82	81	79	78	77	16
17	100	100	99	98	97	96	96	95	94	93	92	91	90	89	88	87	86	85	84	84	83	81	80	79	17
18	102	101	100	100	99	98	97	96	96	95	94	93	92	91	90	89	88	87	86	85	84	83	82	81	18
19	103	103	102	101	100	100	99	98	97	96	95	95	94	93	92	91	90	89	88	87	86	84	84	83	19
20	105	104	104	103	102	101	100	100	99	98	97	96	95	95	94	92	92	91	90	89	88	86	85	84	20
21	107	106	105	104	104	103	102	101	100	100	99	98	97	96	95	94	93	92	91	91	90	88	87	86	21
22	108	108	107	106	105	104	104	103	102	101	100	100	99	98	97	96	95	94	93	92	91	90	89	88	22
23	110	109	109	108	107	106	105	104	104	103	102	101	100	100	99	98	97	96	95	94	93	91	90	90	23
24	112	111	110	110	109	108	107	106	105	105	104	103	102	101	100	100	99	98	97	96	95	93	92	91	24
25	113	113	112	111	111	110	109	108	107	106	106	105	104	103	102	101	100	99	99	98	97	95	94	93	25

Age in years and completed months

Award < 69 for all scores in this area

Raw score	Age in years and completed months																						Raw score
	8:3	8:4	8:5	8:6	8:7	8:8	8:9	8:10	8:11	9:0	9:1	9:2	9:3	9:4	9:5	9:6	9:7	9:8	9:9	9:10	9:11	10:0	10:1	10:2	
26	115	114	114	113	112	112	111	110	109	108	107	107	106	105	104	103	102	101	100	99	98	97	96	95	26
27	117	116	115	115	114	113	113	112	111	110	109	108	107	107	106	105	104	103	102	101	100	98	98	97	27
28	119	118	117	117	116	115	114	114	113	112	111	110	110	109	108	107	106	105	104	103	102	100	99	98	28
29	121	120	120	119	118	117	116	115	115	114	113	112	112	111	110	109	108	107	106	105	104	102	101	100	29
30	123	122	122	121	120	119	119	118	117	116	115	114	114	113	112	111	110	109	108	107	106	104	103	102	30
31	125	125	124	123	122	122	121	120	119	118	117	117	116	115	114	113	112	111	110	109	108	106	105	104	31
32	128	127	126	126	125	124	123	122	122	121	120	119	118	117	116	115	114	113	112	112	111	108	107	106	32
33		130	129	129	128	127	126	125	124	123	123	122	121	120	119	118	117	116	115	114	113	111	110	109	33
34					131	130	129	128	127	126	125	124	123	123	122	121	120	119	118	116	115	113	112	111	34
35									131	130	129	128	127	126	125	124	123	122	121	119	118	116	115	114	35
36			Award > 131 for all scores in this area										131	129	128	127	126	125	124	123	122	119	118	117	36
37																	130	129	128	127	125	123	122	120	37
38																					130	127	126	124	38
39																								130	39
40																									40
	8:3	8:4	8:5	8:6	8:7	8:8	8:9	8:10	8:11	9:0	9:1	9:2	9:3	9:4	9:5	9:6	9:7	9:8	9:9	9:10	9:11	10:0	10:1	10:2	

6 Standardised score tables

PUMA 4 Spring: Age-standardised scores

Raw score	8:7	8:8	8:9	8:10	8:11	9:0	9:1	9:2	9:3	9:4	9:5	9:6	9:7	9:8	9:9	9:10	9:11	10:0	10:1	10:2	10:3	10:4	10:5	10:6	10:7	Raw score
1																										1
2	72	69																								2
3	77	75	72																							3
4	81	78	76	74	71																					4
5	83	81	80	78	76	73	71																			5
6	85	83	82	81	79	77	75	73	71																	6
7	87	85	84	83	82	80	79	77	75	73	71															7
8	89	87	86	85	84	82	81	80	78	76	74	72	70													8
9	90	89	88	87	85	84	83	82	81	79	78	76	74	72	70											9
10	92	91	90	88	87	86	85	84	83	82	80	79	77	76	74	72	70									10
11	94	93	91	90	89	88	87	85	84	83	82	81	80	78	77	75	73	72	70							11
12	95	94	93	92	91	90	88	87	86	85	84	83	82	81	79	78	76	75	73	71	70					12
13	97	96	95	94	93	91	90	89	88	87	86	84	83	82	81	80	79	77	76	74	73	71				13
14	98	97	96	95	94	93	92	91	90	88	87	86	85	84	83	82	81	80	78	77	76	74	72	71	69	14
15	99	98	98	97	96	95	94	92	91	90	89	88	87	86	85	84	83	82	81	79	78	77	75	74	72	15
16	101	100	99	98	97	96	95	94	93	92	91	90	88	87	86	85	84	83	82	81	80	79	78	76	75	16
17	102	101	100	99	99	98	97	96	95	94	92	91	90	89	88	87	86	85	84	83	82	81	80	78	77	17
18	103	102	101	101	100	99	98	97	96	95	94	93	92	91	90	88	87	86	85	84	83	82	81	80	79	18
19	104	104	103	102	101	100	100	99	98	97	96	95	94	92	91	90	89	88	87	86	85	84	83	82	81	19
20	106	105	104	103	102	102	101	100	99	98	97	96	95	94	93	92	91	90	88	87	86	85	84	83	83	20
21	107	106	105	105	104	103	102	101	100	100	99	98	97	96	95	93	92	91	90	89	88	87	86	85	84	21
22	108	108	107	106	105	104	103	103	102	101	100	99	98	97	96	95	94	93	92	91	90	88	87	86	85	22

Award <69 for all scores in this area

Age in years and completed months

Raw score	8:7	8:8	8:9	8:10	8:11	9:0	9:1	9:2	9:3	9:4	9:5	9:6	9:7	9:8	9:9	9:10	9:11	10:0	10:1	10:2	10:3	10:4	10:5	10:6	10:7	Raw score
23	110	109	108	108	107	106	105	104	103	102	101	101	100	99	98	97	96	95	93	92	91	90	89	88	87	23
24	111	110	110	109	108	107	106	105	105	104	103	102	101	100	99	98	97	96	95	94	93	92	91	89	88	24
25	113	112	111	110	110	109	108	107	106	105	104	103	102	101	101	100	99	98	97	96	94	93	92	91	90	25
26	114	113	113	112	111	110	110	109	108	107	106	105	104	103	102	101	100	99	98	97	96	95	94	93	92	26
27	116	115	114	114	113	112	111	110	109	109	108	107	106	105	104	103	102	101	100	99	98	97	96	94	93	27
28	117	117	116	115	115	114	113	112	111	110	109	108	107	106	105	104	103	102	101	100	99	98	97	96	95	28
29	118	118	117	117	116	116	115	114	113	112	111	110	109	108	107	106	105	104	103	102	101	100	99	98	97	29
30	120	119	119	118	118	117	116	116	115	114	113	112	111	110	109	108	107	106	105	103	102	101	100	99	98	30
31	122	121	121	120	119	119	118	117	117	116	115	114	113	112	111	110	109	108	107	105	104	103	102	101	100	31
32	124	123	123	122	121	120	120	119	118	118	117	116	115	114	113	112	111	110	109	108	106	105	104	103	101	32
33	126	125	125	124	123	123	122	121	120	119	119	118	117	117	116	115	113	112	111	110	109	107	106	105	103	33
34	128	128	127	126	126	125	124	124	123	122	121	120	119	119	118	117	116	115	113	112	111	110	108	107	105	34
35		130	130	129	129	128	127	126	125	125	124	123	122	121	120	119	118	117	116	115	114	112	111	109	108	35
36						131	130	130	129	128	127	126	125	124	123	122	121	120	119	118	117	116	114	112	111	36
37											131	130	129	128	127	126	125	124	122	121	120	118	117	116	114	37
38																131	130	128	127	126	124	123	121	119	118	38
39																					130	129	127	125	123	39
40																								130	129	40
Raw score	8:7	8:8	8:9	8:10	8:11	9:0	9:1	9:2	9:3	9:4	9:5	9:6	9:7	9:8	9:9	9:10	9:11	10:0	10:1	10:2	10:3	10:4	10:5	10:6	10:7	

Award >131 for all scores in this area

6 Standardised score tables

PUMA 4 Summer: Age-standardised scores

Raw score	8:10	8:11	9:0	9:1	9:2	9:3	9:4	9:5	9:6	9:7	9:8	9:9	9:10	9:11	10:0	10:1	10:2	10:3	10:4	10:5	10:6	10:7	10:8	10:9	10:10	Raw score
1																										1
2																										2
3	70																									3
4	72	71	70																							4
5	75	74	73	71	70	69																				5
6	77	76	75	74	73	72	71	70																		6
7	79	78	77	76	75	74	73	72	71	70																7
8	81	80	79	78	77	77	76	75	74	73	71	70	69													8
9	83	82	81	80	79	79	78	77	76	75	74	73	72	71	70											9
10	84	83	83	82	81	80	80	79	78	77	76	75	74	73	72	71	70									10
11	86	85	84	84	83	82	81	81	80	79	78	77	76	76	75	74	73	71	70	69						11
12	88	87	86	85	84	84	83	82	82	81	80	79	78	77	77	76	75	74	73	72	71	70				12
13	89	88	88	87	86	85	85	84	83	82	82	81	80	79	78	78	77	76	75	74	73	72	71	70	69	13
14	91	90	89	89	88	87	86	86	85	84	83	83	82	81	80	80	79	78	77	76	75	74	73	72	71	14
15	92	92	91	90	89	89	88	87	86	86	85	84	83	83	82	81	81	80	79	78	77	76	76	75	74	15
16	94	93	93	92	91	90	90	89	88	87	87	86	85	84	84	83	82	81	81	80	79	78	77	77	76	16
17	96	95	94	94	93	92	91	91	90	89	88	88	87	86	85	84	84	83	82	82	81	80	79	78	78	17
18	98	97	96	95	95	94	93	92	91	91	90	89	88	88	87	86	85	85	84	83	82	82	81	80	79	18
19	99	98	98	97	96	96	95	94	93	92	92	91	90	89	89	88	87	86	86	85	84	83	83	82	81	19
20	100	100	99	99	98	97	97	96	95	94	93	93	92	91	90	89	89	88	87	86	86	85	84	83	83	20
21	102	101	101	100	99	99	98	98	97	96	95	94	94	93	92	91	90	90	89	88	87	87	86	85	84	21
22	104	103	102	102	101	100	100	99	99	98	97	96	95	95	94	93	92	91	91	90	89	88	88	87	86	22
23	106	105	104	103	103	102	101	101	100	99	99	98	97	96	96	95	94	93	92	92	91	90	89	88	88	23
24	108	107	107	106	105	104	103	102	102	101	100	100	99	98	98	97	96	95	94	93	93	92	91	90	89	24

Age in years and completed months

Award <69 for all scores in this area

Age in years and completed months

Raw score	8:10	8:11	9:0	9:1	9:2	9:3	9:4	9:5	9:6	9:7	9:8	9:9	9:10	9:11	10:0	10:1	10:2	10:3	10:4	10:5	10:6	10:7	10:8	10:9	10:10	Raw score
25	109	109	108	108	107	106	105	104	103	103	102	101	101	100	99	99	98	97	96	95	94	94	93	92	91	25
26	111	111	110	109	109	108	107	107	106	105	104	103	102	102	101	100	99	99	98	97	96	96	95	94	93	26
27	113	112	112	111	110	110	109	109	108	107	107	106	105	104	103	102	101	100	100	99	98	98	97	96	95	27
28	115	115	114	113	112	112	111	110	110	109	108	108	107	106	105	104	103	102	102	101	100	99	99	98	97	28
29	117	117	116	115	115	114	113	112	112	111	110	110	109	108	108	107	106	105	104	103	102	101	100	100	99	29
30	120	119	118	118	117	116	115	115	114	113	112	112	111	110	109	109	108	107	106	106	104	103	102	101	101	30
31	123	122	121	120	119	119	118	117	116	116	115	114	113	112	112	111	110	109	109	108	107	106	105	104	103	31
32	125	125	124	123	122	122	121	120	119	118	117	117	116	115	114	113	112	111	111	110	109	108	108	107	106	32
33	128	128	127	126	125	125	124	123	122	121	120	119	118	118	117	116	115	114	113	112	111	111	110	109	108	33
34		131	130	129	128	128	127	126	125	124	124	123	122	121	120	119	118	117	116	115	114	113	112	111	110	34
35							130	129	129	128	127	126	125	124	123	122	121	120	119	118	117	116	115	114	113	35
36											130	130	129	128	127	126	125	124	123	122	121	120	119	118	116	36
37															131	130	129	128	127	126	125	124	123	121	120	37
38						Award >131 for all the scores in this area														130	129	128	127	126	125	38
39																								131	130	39
40																										40
	8:10	8:11	9:0	9:1	9:2	9:3	9:4	9:5	9:6	9:7	9:8	9:9	9:10	9:11	10:0	10:1	10:2	10:3	10:4	10:5	10:6	10:7	10:8	10:9	10:10	

6 Standardised score tables

PUMA 5 Autumn: Age-standardised scores

Raw score	Age in years and completed months																						Raw score
	9:3	9:4	9:5	9:6	9:7	9:8	9:9	9:10	9:11	10:0	10:1	10:2	10:3	10:4	10:5	10:6	10:7	10:8	10:9	10:10	10:11	11:0	11:1	11:2	11:3	
1	70																									1
2	76	74	73	72	71	70	69																			2
3	79	78	77	76	75	74	73	72																		3
4	82	81	80	79	78	77	76	76	75	74	73	70														4
5	85	84	83	82	81	80	79	78	77	77	76	75	72	71			70	70	69					69		5
6	87	86	85	84	83	82	81	80	79	79	78	77	75	74	73	73	72	72	71	71	70	70	70	71	71	6
7	89	88	87	86	85	84	83	82	81	81	80	79	77	76	76	75	74	74	73	73	72	72	72	73	73	7
8	91	90	88	87	86	85	85	84	83	82	82	81	80	78	77	77	76	76	75	75	74	74	73	75	74	8
9	92	91	90	89	88	87	86	85	85	84	83	83	82	80	79	78	78	77	77	76	76	76	75	76	76	9
10	94	93	92	91	90	89	88	87	86	85	85	84	83	81	81	80	79	79	78	78	77	77	77	77	77	10
11	96	94	93	93	92	91	90	89	88	87	86	85	85	83	82	82	81	80	80	79	79	78	78	79	78	11
12	97	96	95	94	93	92	91	90	89	88	87	87	86	84	83	83	82	82	81	81	80	80	79	80	80	12
13	98	97	97	96	94	93	93	92	91	90	89	88	87	85	85	84	83	83	82	82	81	81	80	81	81	13
14	99	98	98	97	96	95	94	93	92	91	91	90	89	87	86	85	85	84	84	83	83	82	82	82	82	14
15	101	100	99	98	97	96	95	94	94	93	92	91	90	88	87	86	86	85	85	84	84	83	83	83	83	15
16	102	101	100	99	98	98	97	96	95	94	93	92	92	89	89	88	87	86	86	85	85	84	84	84	84	16
17	104	103	102	101	100	99	98	97	96	95	94	94	93	91	90	89	88	88	87	86	86	85	85	85	85	17
18	105	104	103	102	101	100	99	98	97	97	96	95	94	92	91	91	90	89	88	87	87	86	86	86	86	18
19	106	105	104	103	102	101	100	99	99	98	97	96	95	93	92	92	91	90	89	88	88	87	87	87	87	19
20	107	106	105	104	103	103	102	101	100	99	98	97	97	94	94	93	92	91	91	90	89	89	88	88	88	20
21	108	107	106	105	104	104	103	102	101	100	99	98	98	96	95	94	93	93	92	91	90	90	89	90	89	21
22	109	108	107	106	105	105	104	103	102	101	101	100	99	97	96	95	94	94	93	92	92	91	90	91	90	22
23	110	109	108	107	106	106	105	104	103	102	102	101	100	98	97	97	96	95	94	93	93	92	91	92	91	23
24	111	110	109	108	107	107	106	105	105	104	103	102	101	99	98	98	97	96	95	94	95	94	93	93	92	24

Award < 69 for all scores in this area

| Raw score | \multicolumn{25}{c|}{Age in years and completed months} | Raw score |

Raw score	9:3	9:4	9:5	9:6	9:7	9:8	9:9	9:10	9:11	10:0	10:1	10:2	10:3	10:4	10:5	10:6	10:7	10:8	10:9	10:10	10:11	11:0	11:1	11:2	11:3	Raw score
25	112	111	111	110	109	108	108	107	106	105	105	104	103	102	101	100	99	98	98	97	96	95	94	94	93	25
26	113	112	112	111	110	109	108	108	107	106	106	105	104	103	102	101	100	99	99	98	97	96	96	95	94	26
27	114	114	113	112	111	111	110	109	108	107	107	106	105	105	104	103	102	101	100	99	98	97	97	96	95	27
28	115	115	114	113	113	112	112	111	110	109	108	107	106	106	105	104	103	102	101	100	99	98	98	97	96	28
29	116	116	115	114	114	113	113	112	111	110	109	108	107	107	106	105	104	103	102	101	100	99	99	98	97	29
30	117	117	116	116	115	114	114	113	112	111	110	109	108	108	107	106	105	104	103	102	101	100	100	99	98	30
31	119	118	117	117	116	115	115	114	113	112	112	111	110	109	108	107	107	106	105	104	103	102	101	100	99	31
32	120	119	119	118	117	117	116	115	114	114	113	112	111	110	109	109	108	107	106	105	104	104	103	102	101	32
33	121	121	120	119	119	118	117	117	116	115	114	113	113	112	111	110	109	108	107	106	105	105	104	103	102	33
34	123	122	121	121	120	119	118	118	117	116	115	115	114	113	112	111	110	109	109	108	107	106	105	104	104	34
35	124	123	123	122	121	121	120	119	118	118	117	116	115	114	114	113	112	111	110	109	108	107	106	106	105	35
36	125	125	124	124	123	122	121	121	120	119	118	117	117	116	115	114	113	112	111	110	109	108	108	107	106	36
37	127	126	126	125	124	124	123	122	122	121	120	119	118	117	116	116	115	114	113	112	111	110	109	108	107	37
38	129	128	127	127	126	125	125	124	123	122	122	121	120	119	118	117	116	115	114	113	112	111	110	109	108	38
39	130	130	129	129	128	127	127	126	125	124	123	123	122	121	120	119	118	117	116	115	114	113	112	111	110	39
40				130	130	129	128	128	127	126	125	124	124	123	122	121	120	119	118	117	116	115	114	113	112	40
41							130	130	129	128	128	127	126	125	124	123	122	121	120	119	118	117	115	114	113	41
42										130	130	129	128	127	126	125	124	123	122	121	120	119	118	116	115	42
43													131	130	129	128	127	126	125	124	122	121	120	118	117	43
44																131	130	129	128	126	125	124	123	121	120	44
45																			131	130	129	127	126	124	123	45
46			Award > 131 for all scores in this area																				130	128	127	46
47																								130	129	47
48																									130	48
	9:3	9:4	9:5	9:6	9:7	9:8	9:9	9:10	9:11	10:0	10:1	10:2	10:3	10:4	10:5	10:6	10:7	10:8	10:9	10:10	10:11	11:0	11:1	11:2	11:3	

6 Standardised score tables

PUMA 5 Spring: Age-standardised scores

Age in years and completed months

Raw score	9:6	9:7	9:8	9:9	9:10	9:11	10:0	10:1	10:2	10:3	10:4	10:5	10:6	10:7	10:8	10:9	10:10	10:11	11:0	11:1	11:2	11:3	11:4	11:5	11:6	11:7	Raw score
1																											1
2	73	70																									2
3	77	75	72	69																							3
4	80	78	76	74	71																						4
5	83	81	79	77	75	73	70																				5
6	86	84	82	80	78	76	74	72	70																		6
7	88	87	85	83	81	79	77	76	73	71	69																7
8	90	88	87	85	83	81	79	78	76	75	73	71															8
9	92	90	89	87	86	84	82	80	78	77	76	74	72	70													9
10	93	92	90	89	88	86	84	82	81	79	78	76	75	73	71												10
11	95	93	92	90	89	88	86	85	83	81	80	78	77	76	74	72		69									11
12	96	95	93	92	91	89	88	87	85	83	82	80	79	78	76	75	71	72	70								12
13	98	96	95	93	92	91	90	88	87	86	84	82	81	79	78	77	74	74	73	71	70						13
14	99	98	97	95	94	92	91	90	89	88	86	84	83	81	80	79	76	76	75	74	72	71	70				14
15	100	99	98	97	95	94	93	91	90	89	88	86	85	83	82	80	77	78	77	76	75	73	72	71	69		15
16	101	100	99	98	97	95	94	93	91	90	89	88	87	85	84	82	79	80	78	77	76	75	74	73	71	70	16
17	102	101	100	99	98	97	96	94	93	92	90	89	88	87	86	84	81	81	80	79	78	77	76	75	74	72	17
18	103	102	101	100	99	98	97	96	94	93	92	91	89	88	87	86	83	83	82	80	79	78	77	76	75	74	18
19	104	103	102	101	100	99	98	97	96	94	93	92	91	90	89	88	84	85	83	82	81	80	79	78	77	76	19
20	105	104	103	102	101	100	99	98	97	96	94	93	92	91	90	89	86	87	85	84	83	81	80	79	78	77	20
21	106	105	104	103	102	101	100	99	98	97	96	95	93	92	91	90	88	88	87	85	84	83	82	81	80	79	21
22	107	106	105	104	103	102	101	100	100	99	98	96	95	94	92	91	89	89	88	87	86	85	83	82	81	80	22
23	108	107	106	105	104	103	102	101	101	100	99	98	96	95	94	93	91	90	89	88	87	86	85	84	82	81	23
24	109	108	107	106	105	104	103	102	102	101	100	99	98	97	95	94	93	92	90	89	88	87	86	85	84	83	24
25	111	110	108	107	106	105	105	104	103	102	101	100	99	98	97	95	94	93	92	91	90	89	88	87	85	84	25

Award <69 for all scores in this area

Age in years and completed months

Raw score	9:6	9:7	9:8	9:9	9:10	9:11	10:0	10:1	10:2	10:3	10:4	10:5	10:6	10:7	10:8	10:9	10:10	10:11	11:0	11:1	11:2	11:3	11:4	11:5	11:6	11:7	Raw score
26	112	111	110	109	108	107	106	105	104	103	102	101	100	99	98	97	95	94	93	92	91	90	89	88	87	86	26
27	113	112	111	110	109	108	107	106	105	104	103	102	101	100	99	98	97	96	94	93	92	91	90	89	88	87	27
28	114	113	112	111	110	109	108	107	106	105	104	103	102	101	100	99	98	97	96	94	93	92	91	90	89	88	28
29	115	114	113	112	112	111	109	108	107	106	105	104	103	102	101	100	99	98	97	96	94	93	92	91	90	89	29
30	117	116	115	114	113	112	111	110	108	107	106	105	104	103	102	101	100	99	98	97	96	95	93	92	91	90	30
31	118	117	116	115	114	113	112	111	110	109	108	106	105	104	103	102	101	100	99	98	97	96	95	94	93	92	31
32	120	119	118	117	116	116	113	112	111	110	109	108	107	106	104	103	102	101	100	99	99	97	96	95	94	93	32
33	122	120	119	118	117	116	115	114	113	112	111	109	108	107	106	105	104	102	101	101	99	99	98	96	95	94	33
34	124	123	121	120	119	118	116	115	114	113	112	111	110	108	107	106	105	104	103	102	101	100	99	98	96	95	34
35	126	125	123	122	120	119	118	117	116	115	113	112	111	110	108	107	106	105	104	103	102	101	100	99	98	97	35
36	128	127	126	124	123	121	120	118	117	116	115	114	112	111	110	109	107	106	105	104	103	102	101	100	99	98	36
37		130	128	127	125	124	122	121	119	118	117	115	114	113	112	110	109	108	106	105	104	103	102	101	100	99	37
38			131	129	128	126	125	123	122	120	118	117	116	115	113	112	111	109	108	107	105	104	103	102	101	100	38
39					129	129	128	126	124	123	121	119	118	116	115	114	112	111	110	108	107	106	104	103	102	101	39
40							130	129	127	125	124	122	120	118	117	116	114	113	111	110	108	107	106	105	103	102	40
41									130	129	127	125	123	121	119	118	116	115	113	112	110	109	107	106	105	103	41
42											130	128	126	124	122	120	118	117	115	114	112	111	109	107	106	105	42
43													130	128	126	124	121	119	118	116	114	112	111	110	108	106	43
44															129	127	125	123	120	118	117	115	113	111	110	108	44
45																	129	127	124	122	119	117	115	114	112	110	45
46																			129	126	123	120	118	116	114	112	46
47																				131	128	125	122	119	117	115	47
48																						130	127	124	121	118	48
49																								130	127	123	49
50																										130	50
	9:6	9:7	9:8	9:9	9:10	9:11	10:0	10:1	10:2	10:3	10:4	10:5	10:6	10:7	10:8	10:9	10:10	10:11	11:0	11:1	11:2	11:3	11:4	11:5	11:6	11:7	

Award >131 for all scores in this area

6 Standardised score tables

PUMA 5 Summer: Age-standardised scores

Raw score	9:10	9:11	10:0	10:1	10:2	10:3	10:4	10:5	10:6	10:7	10:8	10:9	10:10	10:11	11:0	11:1	11:2	11:3	11:4	11:5	11:6	11:7	11:8	11:9	11:10	Raw score
1																										1
2	73	71	69																							2
3	77	76	75	73	71	70																				3
4	81	79	78	77	76	75	73	72	70																	4
5	83	82	81	80	78	77	76	75	74	73	72	70	69													5
6	85	84	83	82	81	80	79	78	77	76	75	74	73	72	71	70										6
7	87	86	85	84	83	82	81	80	79	78	77	77	76	75	74	73	72	71	70							7
8	89	88	87	86	85	84	83	82	81	80	79	79	78	77	76	76	75	74	73	72	71	70	69			8
9	91	90	89	88	87	86	85	84	83	82	81	80	80	79	78	77	77	76	75	75	74	73	72	71	70	9
10	92	91	90	89	88	87	86	85	85	84	83	82	81	81	80	79	78	78	77	76	76	75	74	73	73	10
11	94	93	92	91	90	89	88	87	86	85	84	84	83	82	81	81	80	79	79	78	77	77	76	76	75	11
12	95	94	93	92	91	90	89	89	88	87	86	85	84	84	83	82	81	81	80	79	79	78	78	77	76	12
13	97	96	95	94	93	92	91	90	89	88	87	87	86	85	84	84	83	82	82	81	80	80	79	78	78	13
14	98	97	96	95	94	93	92	91	90	90	89	88	87	86	86	85	84	84	83	82	82	81	80	80	79	14
15	99	98	97	97	96	95	94	93	92	91	90	89	88	88	87	86	86	85	84	83	83	82	82	81	80	15
16	100	99	99	98	97	96	95	94	93	92	91	91	90	89	88	88	87	86	85	85	84	83	83	82	82	16
17	102	101	100	99	98	97	96	96	95	94	93	92	91	90	90	89	88	87	87	86	85	85	84	83	83	17
18	103	102	101	100	99	98	98	97	96	95	94	93	92	91	91	90	89	89	88	87	86	86	85	85	84	18
19	104	103	102	101	100	100	99	98	97	96	95	95	94	93	92	91	90	90	89	88	88	87	86	86	85	19
20	105	105	104	103	102	101	100	99	98	98	97	96	95	94	93	92	91	91	90	89	89	88	87	87	86	20
21	106	106	105	104	103	102	101	100	99	99	98	97	96	95	95	94	93	92	91	90	90	89	88	88	87	21
22	107	107	106	105	104	104	103	102	101	100	99	98	97	97	96	95	94	93	92	92	91	90	90	89	88	22
23	109	108	107	106	105	105	104	103	102	101	100	99	98	98	97	96	95	94	94	93	92	91	91	90	89	23
24	110	109	108	107	106	106	105	104	103	102	101	100	100	99	98	97	96	96	95	94	93	92	92	91	90	24
25	111	110	109	109	108	107	106	105	105	104	103	102	101	100	99	98	98	97	96	95	94	94	93	92	91	25
26	112	111	111	110	109	108	107	106	106	105	104	103	102	101	100	99	99	98	97	96	96	95	94	93	92	26
27	113	112	112	111	110	109	108	108	107	106	105	104	103	102	101	101	100	99	98	97	97	96	95	94	94	27

Age in years and completed months

Award <69 for all scores in this area

6 Standardised score tables

Age in years and completed months

Raw score	9:10	9:11	10:0	10:1	10:2	10:3	10:4	10:5	10:6	10:7	10:8	10:9	10:10	10:11	11:0	11:1	11:2	11:3	11:4	11:5	11:6	11:7	11:8	11:9	11:10	Raw score
28	114	113	113	112	111	111	110	109	108	107	106	105	105	104	103	102	101	100	99	99	98	97	96	96	95	28
29	115	114	114	113	112	112	111	110	109	108	107	107	106	105	104	103	102	101	100	100	99	98	97	97	96	29
30	116	116	115	114	113	113	112	111	111	110	109	108	107	106	105	105	104	103	102	101	100	99	98	98	97	30
31	118	117	116	115	115	114	113	112	112	111	110	109	108	107	106	106	105	104	103	102	101	100	99	98	98	31
32	119	119	118	117	116	115	114	114	113	112	111	110	110	109	108	107	106	105	104	104	102	101	100	99	99	32
33	121	120	119	118	117	116	115	115	114	113	112	112	111	110	109	108	107	106	105	105	104	103	102	101	100	33
34	122	121	121	120	119	118	117	116	115	114	114	113	112	111	110	109	108	107	107	106	105	104	103	102	101	34
35	123	123	122	121	120	120	119	118	117	116	115	114	113	112	112	111	110	109	108	107	106	105	104	104	103	35
36	125	124	123	123	122	121	120	119	118	117	116	115	115	114	113	112	111	110	109	108	107	106	106	105	104	36
37	126	125	125	124	123	122	122	121	120	119	118	117	116	115	114	113	112	112	111	110	109	108	107	106	105	37
38	128	127	126	126	125	124	123	122	122	121	120	119	118	117	116	115	114	113	112	111	110	109	108	107	106	38
39	130	129	128	128	127	126	125	124	123	122	121	121	120	119	119	118	117	116	115	114	113	112	110	109	108	39
40			130	129	129	128	127	126	125	124	123	122	121	120	119	118	117	116	115	114	113	112	111	110	109	40
41				131	131	130	129	128	127	126	125	124	123	122	121	120	119	118	117	115	114	113	113	112	111	41
42								130	129	128	127	126	125	124	123	122	121	120	119	118	116	115	114	113	112	42
43										130	129	128	127	126	125	124	123	122	121	120	118	117	116	115	114	43
44													130	129	128	126	125	124	123	122	121	119	118	117	115	44
45															130	129	128	126	125	124	123	122	120	119	118	45
46																	131	129	128	127	125	124	123	121	120	46
47																				130	128	127	125	124	123	47
48																						130	129	127	125	48
49																									129	49
50																										50
	9:10	9:11	10:0	10:1	10:2	10:3	10:4	10:5	10:6	10:7	10:8	10:9	10:10	10:11	11:0	11:1	11:2	11:3	11:4	11:5	11:6	11:7	11:8	11:9	11:10	

Award >131 for all scores in this area

6 Standardised score tables

PUMA 6 Autumn: Age-standardised scores

Raw score	10:1	10:2	10:3	10:4	10:5	10:6	10:7	10:8	10:9	10:10	10:11	11:0	11:1	11:2	11:3	11:4	11:5	11:6	11:7	11:8	11:9	11:10	11:11	12:0	12:1	12:2	Raw score
1																											1
2																											2
3																											3
4									70	70	70	70	70	70	70	70											4
5	74	74	74	71	71	71	71	70	70	73	72	72	72	72	72	72	69	69	69								5
6	77	77	76	76	76	76	73	73	73	75	75	75	74	74	74	74	72	72	71	71					71	71	6
7	79	79	79	79	78	78	78	78	75	75	77	77	77	76	76	76	74	74	73	73	73	73	73	73	73	73	7
8	81	81	81	81	81	81	80	80	77	77	79	79	79	79	78	78	76	76	76	75	75	75	75	75	75	74	8
9	83	82	82	82	82	82	82	81	80	79	79	81	81	81	80	80	78	78	77	77	77	77	77	77	76	76	9
10	84	84	83	83	83	83	83	83	81	81	81	81	82	82	82	81	80	80	79	79	79	79	79	78	78	78	10
11	85	85	85	84	84	84	84	84	82	82	82	82	83	83	83	82	81	81	81	81	81	81	81	80	80	80	11
12	87	87	87	86	86	86	85	85	85	83	83	83	83	83	83	83	82	82	82	82	82	82	82	81	81	81	12
13	89	89	88	88	88	88	87	87	86	84	84	84	84	84	84	84	83	83	83	83	83	83	83	82	82	82	13
14	90	90	90	90	89	89	89	88	88	86	86	85	85	85	85	84	84	84	84	84	84	84	84	83	83	83	14
15	92	91	91	91	91	90	90	90	88	88	88	87	87	87	86	86	86	85	85	85	85	86	86	85	85	85	15
16	93	93	92	92	92	92	91	90	90	89	89	89	89	88	88	88	87	87	87	87	86	86	86	87	87	86	16
17	94	94	93	93	93	93	92	91	91	91	90	90	90	90	89	89	89	89	88	88	88	88	88	88	88	88	17
18	95	95	94	94	94	94	93	93	92	92	91	91	91	91	91	90	90	90	90	89	89	89	89	90	89	89	18
19	97	96	96	96	95	95	94	94	93	93	93	92	92	92	92	91	91	91	91	91	90	90	90	91	90	90	19
20	98	97	97	97	97	96	96	96	94	94	93	93	93	93	93	92	92	92	92	92	91	91	91	92	91	91	20
21	99	99	98	98	98	97	97	97	96	95	94	94	94	94	93	93	93	93	93	92	92	92	92	93	92	92	21
22	100	100	100	99	99	99	98	98	98	97	96	96	95	95	95	94	94	94	94	93	93	93	93	93	93	93	22
23	102	102	101	101	100	100	99	99	99	98	97	97	97	96	96	96	95	95	95	94	94	94	94	94	94	94	23
24	103	103	103	102	102	102	101	101	100	100	98	98	98	97	97	97	96	96	96	96	95	95	95	96	95	95	24
25	104	104	104	103	103	103	102	102	102	101	101	100	100	99	99	99	99	98	98	98	97	97	97	97	96	96	25

Award < 69 for all scores in this area

6 Standardised score tables

Age in years and completed months

Raw score	10:1	10:2	10:3	10:4	10:5	10:6	10:7	10:8	10:9	10:10	10:11	11:0	11:1	11:2	11:3	11:4	11:5	11:6	11:7	11:8	11:9	11:10	11:11	12:0	12:1	12:2	Raw score
26	106	105	105	105	104	104	103	103	103	103	102	102	102	101	101	100	100	99	99	99	98	98	98	98	97	97	26
27	107	107	106	106	106	105	105	104	104	104	103	103	103	102	102	102	101	101	101	100	100	99	99	99	98	98	27
28	108	108	107	107	107	106	106	106	105	105	104	104	104	103	103	103	103	102	102	102	101	101	100	100	100	99	28
29	109	109	109	108	108	108	107	107	107	106	106	105	105	105	104	104	104	103	103	103	102	102	102	102	101	101	29
30	110	110	110	109	109	109	108	108	108	107	107	107	106	106	106	105	105	104	104	104	103	103	103	103	102	102	30
31	111	111	111	111	111	110	110	109	109	109	108	108	107	107	107	106	106	106	105	105	105	104	104	104	103	103	31
32	112	112	112	112	111	111	111	110	110	110	109	109	109	108	108	108	107	107	107	106	106	106	105	105	104	104	32
33	113	113	112	112	112	112	111	111	111	111	110	110	110	109	109	109	108	108	108	107	107	107	106	106	106	105	33
34	115	114	114	113	113	113	112	112	112	112	111	111	111	111	110	110	110	109	109	109	108	108	108	107	107	107	34
35	116	116	116	115	115	114	114	113	113	112	112	112	112	111	111	111	111	110	110	110	109	109	109	108	108	108	35
36	118	118	117	117	116	116	115	115	114	114	113	113	112	112	112	112	111	111	111	111	110	110	110	109	109	109	36
37	120	119	119	118	118	117	117	116	116	115	115	114	114	113	113	113	112	112	112	112	111	111	111	111	110	110	37
38	122	121	121	120	120	119	119	118	118	117	117	116	116	115	115	114	114	113	113	112	112	112	112	111	111	111	38
39	124	123	123	122	121	121	120	120	119	119	118	118	117	117	116	116	115	115	114	114	113	113	112	112	112	112	39
40	126	125	124	124	123	123	122	122	121	121	120	119	119	118	118	117	117	116	116	115	115	114	114	113	113	113	40
41	128	128	127	126	125	125	124	124	123	123	122	121	121	120	120	119	119	118	118	117	117	116	116	115	115	114	41
42	131	130	129	129	128	127	127	126	125	124	124	123	123	122	122	121	120	120	119	119	118	118	117	117	116	116	42
43					130	130	129	128	128	127	126	125	125	124	124	123	122	122	121	121	120	120	119	118	118	117	43
44									130	129	129	128	127	127	126	125	124	124	123	123	122	122	121	120	120	119	44
45												131	130	129	128	128	127	126	126	125	124	124	123	122	122	121	45
46			Award > 131 for all scores in this area													130	130	129	128	127	127	126	125	124	124	123	46
47																				130	129	129	128	127	126	126	47
48																							131	130	129	128	48
49																										131	49
50																											50
	10:1	10:2	10:3	10:4	10:5	10:6	10:7	10:8	10:9	10:10	10:11	11:0	11:1	11:2	11:3	11:4	11:5	11:6	11:7	11:8	11:9	11:10	11:11	12:0	12:1	12:2	

PUMA 6 *Spring*: Age-standardised scores

Award <70 for all scores in this area (upper right blank region).

Raw score	10:4	10:5	10:6	10:7	10:8	10:9	10:10	10:11	11:0	11:1	11:2	11:3	11:4	11:5	11:6	11:7	11:8	11:9	11:10	11:11	12:0	12:1	12:2	12:3	12:4	12:5	12:6	Raw score
1																												1
2	72																											2
3	75	72																										3
4	76	75	71																									4
5	78	76	75	71																								5
6	79	78	76	74	71																							6
7	81	79	78	76	74	71																						7
8	82	81	79	78	76	74	71	70																				8
9	83	82	81	79	78	76	74	71	70																			9
10	85	84	82	81	80	78	76	74	70																			10
11	86	85	84	83	81	80	78	76	74	74																		11
12	87	86	85	84	83	81	80	78	76	76	73																	12
13	88	87	86	85	84	83	81	80	78	78	77	73																13
14	89	88	87	86	84	85	83	82	80	80	79	77	73															14
15	91	90	88	87	86	85	85	84	82	82	81	79	77	72														15
16	92	91	89	88	87	86	86	85	84	84	83	81	79	77	72													16
17	94	93	92	91	90	89	88	87	86	86	85	83	81	79	77	72												17
18	95	94	93	93	92	90	89	88	87	87	86	85	83	81	79	77	71											18
19	96	95	95	94	93	92	91	90	89	89	88	87	85	84	82	80	77	71										19
20	97	96	96	95	94	94	93	92	90	91	90	88	87	86	84	82	80	77	70									20
21	98	97	97	96	96	95	94	93	92	93	92	90	89	88	86	85	82	80	77									21
22	99	98	98	97	97	96	96	95	94	95	94	93	91	90	88	87	85	83	80	77								22
23	99	99	99	98	98	97	97	96	95	96	95	94	93	92	90	89	87	86	83	80	77							23
24	100	100	99	99	99	99	98	98	97	97	97	96	95	94	93	91	89	88	86	84	81	77						24
25	100	100	100	100	99	99	99	99	98	98																		25

Age in years and completed months

Raw score	10:4	10:5	10:6	10:7	10:8	10:9	10:10	10:11	11:0	11:1	11:2	11:3	11:4	11:5	11:6	11:7	11:8	11:9	11:10	11:11	12:0	12:1	12:2	12:3	12:4	12:5	12:6	Raw score
26	101	101	101	100	100	100	99	99	99	98	98	97	96	96	95	93	92	90	89	87	85	81	80	77				26
27	102	102	101	101	101	100	100	100	99	99	99	98	98	97	96	95	94	93	91	89	87	85	82	80	77			27
28	103	102	102	102	101	101	101	100	100	100	99	99	99	98	98	97	96	95	94	92	90	88	86	83	80	77		28
29	104	104	103	103	102	102	102	101	101	100	100	100	99	99	99	98	98	97	96	95	93	92	89	87	84	80	75	29
30	106	105	104	104	103	103	102	102	102	101	101	101	100	100	99	99	99	98	98	97	96	94	93	90	88	85	77	30
31	107	107	106	105	105	104	104	103	103	102	102	101	101	101	100	100	100	99	99	98	97	97	95	94	92	89	86	31
32	109	108	108	107	106	106	105	104	104	103	103	102	102	101	101	101	100	100	100	99	99	98	97	96	95	93	90	32
33	111	110	109	109	108	107	107	106	105	105	104	104	103	103	102	102	101	101	100	100	100	99	99	98	97	96	95	33
34	113	112	111	110	110	109	108	108	107	106	106	105	104	104	103	103	102	102	101	101	101	100	99	99	98	98	97	34
35	116	114	113	112	112	111	110	109	109	108	108	107	106	105	105	104	104	103	102	102	102	101	100	99	99	99	99	35
36	118	117	116	115	114	113	112	111	111	110	109	109	108	107	106	106	105	104	104	103	103	102	102	101	100	100	100	36
37	121	119	118	117	116	115	114	113	112	112	111	110	110	109	108	108	107	106	105	105	104	104	103	102	101	101	101	37
38	125	123	121	120	119	118	117	116	115	114	113	112	111	111	110	109	109	108	107	107	106	105	104	104	103	103	102	38
39		129	125	123	122	120	119	118	117	116	115	114	113	113	112	111	110	110	109	108	108	107	106	105	105	104	104	39
40			129	126	126	124	122	121	119	118	117	117	116	115	114	113	112	111	111	110	109	109	108	107	107	106	105	40
41				129	130	130	126	124	122	121	120	119	118	117	116	115	114	113	113	112	111	110	110	109	108	108	107	41
42							126	125	130	124	123	121	120	119	118	117	116	116	115	114	113	112	112	111	110	109	109	42
43											127	124	123	122	121	119	118	118	117	116	115	114	113	113	112	111	110	43
44										130		130	127	125	123	122	121	120	119	118	117	116	116	115	114	113	112	44
45														130	128	125	124	122	121	120	119	118	117	117	116	115	114	45
46																131	128	125	124	123	121	120	119	119	118	117	116	46
47																		128	128	126	124	123	122	121	120	119	118	47
48																					128	126	124	123	122	121	120	48
49																							129	126	124	123	122	49
50																								129	127	125	50
	10:4	10:5	10:6	10:7	10:8	10:9	10:10	10:11	11:0	11:1	11:2	11:3	11:4	11:5	11:6	11:7	11:8	11:9	11:10	11:11	12:0	12:1	12:2	12:3	12:4	12:5	12:6	

Award >131 for all scores in this area

PUMA 6 Summer: Age-standardised scores

Raw score	10:3	10:4	10:5	10:6	10:7	10:8	10:9	10:10	10:11	11:0	11:1	11:2	11:3	11:4	11:5	11:6	11:7	11:8	11:9	11:10	11:11	12:0	12:1	12:2	12:3	12:4	12:5	12:6	12:7	Raw score
1																														1
2																														2
3																														3
4																														4
5																														5
6																														6
7																														7
8																														8
9																														9
10	74	71																												10
11	82	80	78	75	72	70																								11
12	86	85	83	82	80	78	76	74	71																					12
13	90	88	87	86	84	83	82	80	78	77	75	72	70																	13
14	93	92	91	89	87	86	85	84	83	81	80	78	77	75	73	72	70													14
15	96	94	93	92	91	89	88	86	85	84	83	82	81	80	79	77	76	74	73	71	69									15
16	99	97	96	94	93	92	91	89	88	87	86	85	84	83	82	81	80	79	77	76	75	73	72	70						16
17	102	100	98	97	95	94	93	92	91	90	88	87	86	85	84	84	83	82	81	80	79	78	76	75	74	73	71	70		17
18	105	103	101	99	98	96	95	94	93	92	91	90	89	88	87	86	85	84	83	82	82	81	80	79	78	77	76	75	73	18
19	107	106	104	102	100	99	97	96	95	94	93	92	91	90	89	88	87	86	85	84	84	83	82	81	81	80	79	78	77	19
20	110	108	106	105	103	101	100	98	97	96	95	94	93	92	91	90	89	88	87	86	86	85	84	83	83	82	82	81	80	20
21	114	111	109	107	106	104	102	101	99	98	97	96	95	94	93	92	91	90	89	88	87	87	86	85	85	84	83	83	82	21
22	116	114	112	110	108	106	105	103	102	100	99	97	96	95	94	94	93	92	91	90	89	88	87	87	86	86	85	85	84	22
23	121	117	115	113	111	108	107	106	104	102	101	100	98	97	96	95	94	94	93	92	92	91	90	89	88	87	86	86	85	23
24	128	122	118	115	114	112	109	107	106	105	103	102	100	99	98	97	96	95	94	94	93	92	92	91	90	89	88	87	87	24
25		130	123	119	116	114	113	110	108	107	106	104	102	101	100	99	98	97	96	95	94	93	93	92	92	91	90	89	88	25

Award <69 for all scores in this area

Age in years and completed months

Raw score	10:3	10:4	10:5	10:6	10:7	10:8	10:9	10:10	10:11	11:0	11:1	11:2	11:3	11:4	11:5	11:6	11:7	11:8	11:9	11:10	11:11	12:0	12:1	12:2	12:3	12:4	12:5	12:6	12:7	Raw score
26			124																										90	26
27					120																							91	92	27
28						117	115	113	111	109	107	106	105	103	102	101	99	98	97	96	96	95	94	93	92	92	92	92	93	28
29					126	121	118	115	114	112	110	108	107	105	104	103	101	100	99	98	97	96	95	95	94	93	93	93	94	29
30						128	122	119	116	114	113	110	109	107	106	105	103	102	101	100	99	98	97	96	95	94	94	94	94	30
31							130	124	119	117	115	113	111	109	108	107	105	104	103	102	100	99	98	97	97	96	95	96	95	31
32									125	120	118	115	114	112	110	108	107	106	105	103	102	101	100	99	98	97	96	96	96	32
33										127	122	118	116	114	113	111	109	107	106	105	104	103	102	101	100	99	98	97	96	33
34											128	123	119	117	115	113	112	110	108	107	106	105	103	102	101	99	99	98	98	34
35												130	124	120	117	115	114	112	110	109	107	106	105	104	103	102	101	100	99	35
36														125	121	118	116	114	113	111	109	108	107	106	105	104	102	101	100	36
37															127	122	119	116	115	113	112	110	108	107	106	105	104	103	102	37
38																129	123	119	117	115	114	113	111	109	108	107	106	105	103	38
39																	130	124	120	118	116	114	113	111	110	109	107	106	105	39
40																			125	121	118	116	115	114	113	111	109	107	107	40
41																				127	122	119	117	115	114	113	111	109	108	41
42																					129	123	120	118	116	115	113	112	110	42
43																						130	124	121	118	117	115	114	112	43
44																								126	122	119	117	115	114	44
45																									127	123	119	117	116	45
46																										129	124	120	118	46
47																											130	125	121	47
48																													126	48
49																														49
50	10:3	10:4	10:5	10:6	10:7	10:8	10:9	10:10	10:11	11:0	11:1	11:2	11:3	11:4	11:5	11:6	11:7	11:8	11:9	11:10	11:11	12:0	12:1	12:2	12:3	12:4	12:5	12:6	12:7	50

Award >130 for all scores in this area

Appendix A: Facilities for each question

Where two values are given, these represent the different parts of the question.

PUMA 3 Autumn		PUMA 3 Spring		PUMA 3 Summer	
Question number	% correct	Question number	% correct	Question number	% correct
1	94	1	77	1	98
2	51	2	73		95
3	88	3	88	2	51
4	77		82		47
5a	61	4	71	3	49
5b	45	5a	75	4	68
6	71	5b	45	5	74
7a	75	6	59	6	74
7b	57	7	78	7	57
8a	74	8	60	8	61
8b	83	9	71	9	79
8c	74	10	58	10	90
9	48	11	23		52
10a	51	12	54	11	80
10b	65	13a	62		50
11	28	13b	34	12	79
12	40	14	33		65
13	53	15	31	13	48
14	75		34	14	38
15	78	16	29		54
	76	17a	86	15	59
16	29	17b	63	16	54
17	52	18	29		43
18	36	19	29	17	57
19	38	20	63		49
20	29	21	46	18a	74
21	55		38	18b	47
	35	22	83	18c	47
22	22	23a	45	19	53
23	31	23b	48	20	35
24	47	23c	35	21	38
25	23	24	28	22	22
26a	16	25	34	23	43
26b	23		30	24	24
27	21	26	42	25	8
	10	27	13		42
28	19	28	41	26	29
	22	29	9	27	20
29	16	30	9	28	14
30	5	31	26	29	11

PUMA 4 Autumn		PUMA 4 Spring		PUMA 4 Summer	
Question number	% correct	Question number	% correct	Question number	% correct
1	91	1	82	1	74
2	86	2	63	2	85
3a	80	3	74	2	72
3b	41	4	87	3	44
4a	90	5	56	4	74
4b	74	6a	84	5	73
5	42	6b	84	6a	81
6	45	7	42	6b	19
7	75	8	30	7	65
8	77	9	49	8	80
9	48	10a	72	9	80
10	62	10b	35	9	82
11	51	10c	62	10	66
12	58	11	53	11	85
13a	43	12	80	12	75
13b	4	13	39	12	63
14	56	14	33	13a	46
15	80	15	52	13b	78
16	75	16a	51	14	52
17a	91	16b	53	15	24
17b	33	17	43	16	26
17c	25	18	46	17	31
18	42	19	29	18	23
19	59	20	21	19	80
20	54	21a	36	20a	78
20	60	21b	26	20b	66
20	41	22	20	20c	71
21	30	23	69	21	21
22	15	23	55	22	10
22	43	24	37	22	37
23	19	24	32	23	21
23	18	25	31	24	64
24	34	25	20	25	69
25	14	26	12	25	41
26	37	27	42	25	36
27	55	28	18	26	42
28	41	29	23	27	21
29a	6	30	35	28	20
29b	8	30	39	29	27
30	10	31	20	29	12

Appendix A: Facilities for each question

PUMA 5 Autumn		PUMA 5 Spring		PUMA 5 Summer	
Question number	% correct	Question number	% correct	Question number	% correct
1	76	1	70	1	77
2	45	2	48	2	74
3a	74	3	78		77
3b	76		78	3	65
4	30	4	64		30
5	74	5	55	4	71
6a	76	6	45	5	44
6b	63	7	52	6	76
7	56	8a	82	7	60
8	30	8b	47		59
9	59	9	62	8	37
10	57	10	59	9	66
11	51	11	44	10	78
12a	37	12	43		35
12b	23	13	63		54
12c	40	14	55		23
13	35	15	47	11	54
14a	90	16	47	12	44
14b	60	17	52	13	24
15	25	18	33	14	60
16a	29		21	15	61
16b	27	19	44	16	42
17a	46	20	47	17	45
17b	19		31	18	27
17c	17	21a	68	19	6
18a	67	21b	39	20	51
18b	37	22	38		45
18c	55		26	21	24
19	33	23	73	22	45
20a	39	24	47	23	45
20b	24	25	23		51
20c	15	26	34	24	19
21	43	27	57	25	25
22	51		20	26	12
23	21	28	33	27	28
24	58	29a	44	28	18
	48	29b	40	29	16

Appendix A: Facilities for each question

PUMA 5 Autumn		PUMA 5 Spring		PUMA 5 Summer	
25	30	30	30	30	21
25	22	31	48	31	26
26a	38	31	14	32a	35
26b	29	32	29	32b	11
27	60	33a	26	33	10
27	17	33b	11	34	50
28a	31	34	35	34	52
28b	14	35a	38	35	14
29	18	35b	11	36	18
30a	47	36	17	37	15
30b	37	37	31	38	24
31	11	38a	34	38	11
32	16	38b	27	39	13

PUMA 6 Autumn		PUMA 6 Spring		PUMA 6 Summer	
Question number	% correct	Question number	% correct	Question number	% correct
1	88	1	83	1	93
2	76	2	85	1	85
3a	78	3	83	2	80
3b	70	4	82	3a	64
4	75	5	70	3b	46
5	62	6	61	4	40
6	76	7	55	5a	69
7	66	8	58	5b	55
8	87	9	79	6	79
8	72	9	66	7	72
9	69	10	50	8	62
10	58	11	69	9	71
11	52	12	69	10a	70
11	32	13	84	10b	49
12	58	14	67	11a	93
13	78	15	81	11b	79
13	63	15	65	11c	84
14	65	16	50	12	64
15a	60	16	36	12	39
15b	41	17	80	13	72
15c	43	18a	72	14	31
15d	5	18b	72	15	37

PUMA 6 Autumn		PUMA 6 Spring		PUMA 6 Summer	
16	76	19	63	16	66
17	42	20	64		49
18a	55	21	70	17a	45
18b	20	22	79	17b	30
19	68	23a	74	18a	45
	45	23b	49	18b	29
20a	47	24a	60	19	42
20b	29	24b	44	20a	29
21	59	25	76	20b	50
22	33		22	21	38
23	48	26	32	22a	61
24	33	27	68	22b	28
25a	57	28a	28	23a	19
25b	58	28b	33	23b	16
26	25	29	26	24	16
27a	10	30a	47	25a	37
27b	28	30b	26	25b	14
28	61	31	22	26	51
	6	32	61		44
29	54		23	27	44
	28	33	14	28a	54
30	18	34a	68	28b	32
31	25	34b	43	29	36
32	16	35	27	30	34
33	10	36a	48	31	8
34a	27	36b	21	32	17
34b	14	36c	5	33	10
35	8	37	24	34	18

Appendix B: Thresholds obtained algorithmically from facilities

Year 3 Autumn			
Raw score range	Performance indicator	Facility range	Number of questions at this facility
0–7	Working towards	90%–100%	1
8–24	Emerging	60%–89%	12
25–35	Expected	20%–59%	22
36–40	Exceeding	0%–19%	5

Year 4 Autumn			
Raw score range	Performance indicator	Facility range	Number of questions at this facility
0–7	Working towards	90%–100%	3
8–22	Emerging	60%–89%	9
23–34	Expected	20%–59%	20
35–40	Exceeding	0%–19%	8

Year 5 Autumn			
Raw score range	Performance indicator	Facility range	Number of questions at this facility
0–5	Working towards	90%–100%	1
6–27	Emerging	60%–89%	9
28–43	Expected	20%–59%	32
44–50	Exceeding	0%–19%	8

Year 6 Autumn			
Raw score range	Performance indicator	Facility range	Number of questions at this facility
0–10	Working towards	90%–100%	0
11–30	Emerging	60%–89%	18
31–43	Expected	20%–59%	24
44–50	Exceeding	0%–19%	8

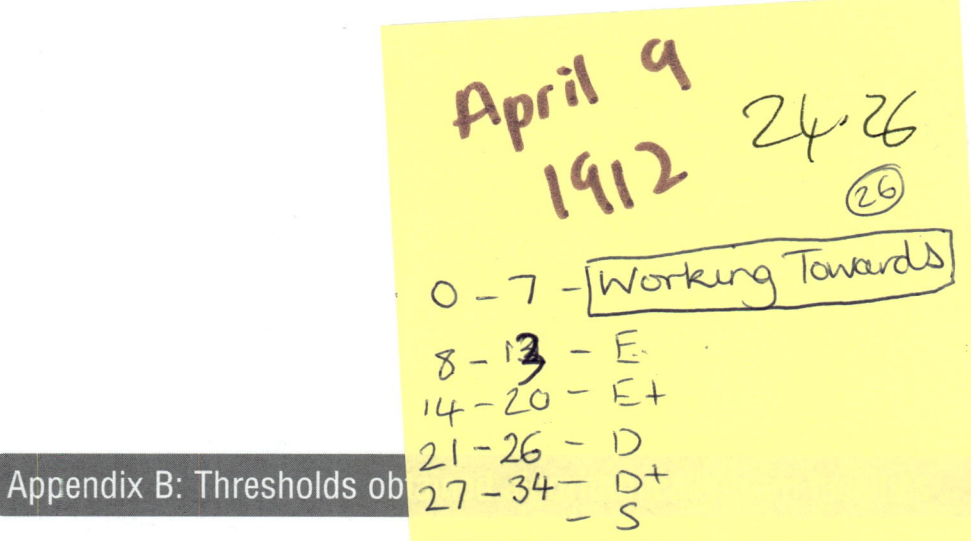

Handwritten note:
April 9 1912 24.26 (26)
0–7 – Working Towards
8–13 – E
14–20 – E+
21–26 – D
27–34 – D+
– S

Year 3 Spring

Raw score range	Performance indicator	Facility range	Number of questions at this facility
0–7	Working towards	90%–100%	0
8–25	Emerging	60%–89%	14
26–36	Expected	20%–59%	23
37–40	Exceeding	0%–19%	3

Year 4 Spring

Raw score range	Performance indicator	Facility range	Number of questions at this facility
0–5	Working towards	90%–100%	0
6–25	Emerging	60%–89%	10
26–35	Expected	20%–59%	28
36–40	Exceeding	0%–19%	2

Year 5 Spring

Raw score range	Performance indicator	Facility range	Number of questions at this facility
0–4	Working towards	90%–100%	0
5–29	Emerging	60%–89%	9
30–44	Expected	20%–59%	37
45–50	Exceeding	0%–19%	4

Year 6 Spring

Raw score range	Performance indicator	Facility range	Number of questions at this facility
0–15	Working towards	90%–100%	0
16–36	Emerging	60%–89%	27
37–46	Expected	20%–59%	21
47–50	Exceeding	0%–19%	2

Appendix B: Thresholds obtained algorithmically from facilities

Year 3 Summer			
Raw score range	Performance indicator	Facility range	Number of questions at this facility
0–8	Working towards	90%–100%	3
9–25	Emerging	60%–89%	9
26–35	Expected	20%–59%	25
36–40	Exceeding	0%–19%	3

Year 4 Summer			
Raw score range	Performance indicator	Facility range	Number of questions at this facility
0–12	Working towards	90%–100%	0
13–28	Emerging	60%–89%	21
29–36	Expected	20%–59%	16
37–40	Exceeding	0%–19%	3

Year 5 Summer			
Raw score range	Performance indicator	Facility range	Number of questions at this facility
0–6	Working towards	90%–100%	0
7–25	Emerging	60%–89%	11
26–42	Expected	20%–59%	27
43–50	Exceeding	0%–19%	12

Year 6 Summer			
Raw score range	Performance indicator	Facility range	Number of questions at this facility
0–10	Working towards	90%–100%	2
11–30	Emerging	60%–89%	16
31–43	Expected	20%–59%	24
44–50	Exceeding	0%–19%	8